Games People Play

The Biggest and Best Book of Party Games and Activities

PENNY WARNER

Meadowbrook Press
Distributed by Simon & Schuster
New York

Library of Congress Cataloging-in-Publication Data

Warner, Penny.
    Games people play : the biggest and best book of party games and
activities / Penny Warner.
        p.   cm.
    ISBN 0-88166-304-2
    1. Indoor games. 2. Entertaining. I. Title.
    GV1471.W268 1997
    793.2—dc21   97-41425
                                                          CIP
Publisher's ISBN: 0-88166-304-2
Simon & Schuster Ordering # 0-671-58001-9

Editor: Liya Lev Oertel
Production Manager: Joe Gagne
Production Assistant: Danielle White
Cover Art: Jack Lindstrom

© 1997 by Penny Warner

All rights reserved. No part of this book may be reproduced or transmitted in
any form or by any means, electronic or mechanical, including photocopying,
recording, or using any information storage and retrieval system without
written permission from the publisher, except in the case of brief quotations
embodied in critical articles and reviews.

Published by Meadowbrook Press, 5451 Smetana Drive, Minnetonka, MN
55343

BOOK TRADE DISTRIBUTION by Simon & Schuster, a division of Simon and
Schuster, Inc., 1230 Avenue of the Americas, New York, NY 10020

00 99 98   10 9 8 7 6 5 4 3 2

Printed in the United States of America

Dedication

To Tom, Matthew, and Rebecca,
who love to play games

Acknowledgments

Thanks for playing with us:
Len and Barbara Swec
Tim, Jana, and Joseph Swec

9-27-01   GIFT   8.00

Table of Contents

Introduction

Just as party food, decorations, and themes have changed over the years, so have party games. Today's party people have grown tired of the same old games. They want activities that are new, challenging, fast-paced, and thought-provoking. They want to go beyond Charades.

Games People Play offers a wide selection of fun and exciting games for grownups: silly games, such as Baby Business, in which players have to identify those bizarre-looking baby gadgets; thinking games, such as Clueless, in which players solve a puzzle with only one clue at a time; physical games, such as Don't Drop It!, in which players have to pass awkward items down the line; and games of chance, such as Bet the Lottery! in which players buy tickets and win prizes—both good and bad—all according to luck.

You'll find old favorites with a twist, such as Monster Movie Charades, in which players act out scenes or monsters from favorite films; or Eyewitness, in which players watch a crime being committed and write down what they see. You'll find new games for the twenty-first century, many adapted from the bestsellers on the game-store shelves, such as Couch Potato, in which players channel surf in search of scavenger-type items; or Draw!, in which your pencil does the work while your teammates guess the answers. You'll also find plenty of old standards that aren't ready to be forgotten, such as Holiday Trivia, in which players need to know the names of the eight reindeer or the ingredients to eggnog; or Lucky Strike, in which players bowl for prizes instead of pins.

Each entry is presented in an easy-to-follow format, with a brief introduction to give you a flavor of the game and a list of materials needed to help you set up the game efficiently and economically. Playing time is suggested, so you know how long the game may last—unless you want to play it over and over again! And a step-by-step how-to-play guide leads you through the game quickly and easily. Also, each game includes a "Variation"—a creative twist on the basic game. With all the games and variations, you'll have over 400 choices for entertaining your guests!

Once you've selected the games you want to play, you can organize your party around them. If you plan to play Lover's Connection, set the mood with romantic decorations, hearts and flowers, and sweet desserts. If your party revolves around the Lip-Sync Contest, use the musical theme for invitations, decorations, food, and favors.

As you plan your guest list, choose games to suit the number of people invited. You may have to adapt some of the games for very small or very large groups, but with creativity and imagination, you can make any of the games work for your crowd.

Some tips before you begin:

- Make sure you have plenty of room to play the games, so that everyone is comfortable during the activities.
- Explain the rules clearly and simply, and agree upon any changes before the game begins. Have a trial run of the game before you officially start, so everyone is familiar with the rules.
- Limit the games to a reasonable length of time, so players don't get bored. Have an extra game or two ready as backup, in case one of the games ends quickly or is not right for your crowd.
- Tell those guests who hate games that these games are new, different, and worth a try. Most people enjoy games that are fresh and unusual because they haven't had past experiences with failure or boredom.
- If there are conflicts, replay a game or round. Vote for changes, if necessary.
- Oversee the games to make sure everyone is included and enjoying the fun. Try to include yourself as much as possible, and avoid being the emcee for every game.
- Have plenty of prizes available for winners—and losers too. Booby prizes and funny gifts are always welcome. Try to make the prize appropriate for the game. For food games, give the winners boxes of candy. For music games, give cassette singles. For picture games, give copies of the picture or poster to take home. Try to keep the gifts genderless, such as boxes of cookies or chocolate, music, travel games, wine, plants, and so on.

Enough with the talk! Let the games begin!

Peggy Warner

Academy Awards

Invite a few movie fans to watch the Academy Awards. Then vote for the most trivial, ludicrous, and just plain silly nominations.

Materials Needed
- Large sheet of poster board
- Felt-tip pens in a variety of colors

Playing Time: 2–3 hours

How to Play

1. Draw a large grid on poster board, with enough rows for each of the nomination categories, and enough columns for each of your guests.

2. Write the nomination categories down the left-hand side of each row, such as Best Picture, Best Actor, Best Actress, and so on. Write the players' names across the top, one name for each column.

3. Also include funny categories, such as Most Embarrassing Speech, Most Boring Speech, Ugliest Outfit, Most Risqué Gown, "Worst Hair Style, Weirdest Walk to the Stage, Oddest Couple, Best Commercial, Funniest Joke by the Emcee, Most Pompous Actor, Most Excited to Win, and Most Blasé about the Awards.

4. Hand out a different color felt-tip pen to each guest and have them write their nominations in the squares next to each category, beneath their own names.

5. As the awards are announced, draw stars on the winning squares.

6. Determine winners at the end of the show.

7. Offer a prize to the player who has the most correct answers.

Variation

Have the guests come dressed as nominated stars, and let the players guess who they are supposed to be. Have the costumed players act out movie scenes to help the other players guess their identity.

Are You Calling Me a Liar?

Did you know Elvis had Madonna's alien baby? Are you calling me a liar? Okay. Would you believe Michael Jackson sleeps in a coffin? Still think I'm lying? Gotcha!

Materials Needed

- Collection of stories from the tabloids
- 30 index cards
- Pen or pencil

Playing Time: 30–45 minutes

How to Play

1. Read the tabloid papers, and gather juicy tidbits about the stars—the more outrageous (but basically true) the better, such as "Woody Harrelson's Father Is a Convict" or "Roseanne Has Reunion with Baby She Gave Up for Adoption."

2. Then make up some phony headlines about the stars, such as "Dolly Parton Has Emergency Breast Enhancement Surgery" or "Brad Pitt Was Once Secretly Engaged to Roseanne."

3. Write ten true headlines on index cards.

4. Write twenty false headlines on index cards. (Indicate on each card whether the headline is false.)

5. Shuffle the cards and give one to each player.

6. Have Player 1 read the headline on his or her card aloud.

7. Have the rest of the players write down whether they think the headline is true (according to the tabloid) or false.

8. Tell the players to read their answers to the group. Give a point for each correct guess.

9. Continue playing until all the players had a chance to read their headlines.

10. If you like, hand out new cards, and play a second round. You may want to determine before the game the number of points necessary to win. The player who gets that many points first wins a prize.

Variation

Read tabloid headlines, but leave out the names of the stars. Have the players guess the stars.

Art School Dropout

You don't have to be an art historian to like this game. All you need is some basic knowledge of famous artworks.

Materials Needed
- Reproductions of famous artwork, available at the library
- Construction paper
- Paper
- Pencils, 1 for each player
- Glue or tape

Playing Time: 30 minutes

How to Play

1. Gather a variety of famous art reproductions from the library. Select twelve to twenty prints. If the prints are in books, photocopy them, using a color copier if possible, and glue or tape them onto construction paper.

2. Cover the name of the artist and the title of the print.

3. Hang the prints along one wall of the party room, like a gallery display.

4. At game time, distribute paper and pencils.

5. Have the players enter the gallery, study the prints, and try to identify them, writing down their answers.

6. After all the players have written their guesses, reveal the answers. Give points for correct names of the artist and/or print, dates, and other details.

7. Award a prize to the player with the most points.

Variation

For an easier version, list the names of the artists on large individual name tags, and place them underneath the prints—incorrectly. Have the players try to match the correct names with the prints.

Baby Business

How well do you know the baby business? Find out fast with this game.

Materials Needed

- A collection of odd-looking or difficult-to-identify baby items, such as a nose syringe, a temperature patch, a bellybutton clip, a bottle brush, a thumb-sucking splint, a breast pump, a baby nail clipper, a harness, an odd toy, a cup lid, and so on
- Paper
- Pencils, 1 for each player
- Baby doll (optional)

Playing Time: 30 minutes

How to Play

1. Assemble your collection of baby items. Baby specialty shops are great resources, and so are friends who have infants. Or, instead of using actual items, use pictures from baby magazines.

2. Arrange the items on a table, with a baby doll propped in the middle for a centerpiece. Offer pencils and paper to the players.

3. Have the players sit in a circle. Pass the objects around the circle, one at a time, so each player can examine them.

4. Tell the players to identify each item and to write down their answers. Funny comments are welcome!

5. After all items have been seen, reveal their names and purposes. Give a point for each correct answer.

6. Award a prize to the player with the most points.

Variation

Instead of using baby items that players can see and touch, use baby items they can only smell. Spoon or squirt a small amount of such things as baby food, diaper rash medicine, teething medicine, baby lotion, Vaseline, and baby cough syrup onto small paper plates. Pass them around and have the players guess each one.

Baby-Food Taste Test

You feed your babies this stuff, but have you ever tasted it? Bet you can't tell one flavor from another! (Is that cat food?!)

Materials Needed

- 8 jars of various baby foods (meat, fruit, vegetable, and cereal)
- Foil
- Felt-tip pen
- Paper plates and plastic spoons, 1 for each player
- Paper
- Pencils, 1 for each player

Playing Time: 30 minutes

How to Play

1. Cover the labels of the baby-food jars with foil, and write a number on the side of each jar with a felt-tip pen: Jar 1, Jar 2, and so on.

2. Give each player a paper plate, spoon, sheet of paper, and pencil.

3. Ask the players to draw eight circles on their plate and to label each with a number just outside the circle.

4. Pass around Jar 1, and have the players spoon out a small amount into Circle 1. Repeat with the other seven jars until all the circles are full.

5. When everyone is served, the players must taste the globs of food, then write down what they think each food is.

6. When all the players have guessed, peel off the foil to reveal the flavors.

7. Award a prize to the player with the best taste buds.

Variation

Have the players guess the flavor by simply smelling the baby food. Or have half the players close their eyes, and have the other half feed them the baby food, so they can't see the color. Then switch sides, and have the feeders close their eyes, so everyone has a chance to taste.

Back Home

When your guests realize they're not in Kansas anymore, can they find their way home again? Where's that yellow brick road?

Materials Needed

- Photocopies of maps: local, national, or international
- Felt-tip pens, 1 for each player

Playing Time: 30 minutes

How to Play

1. Give each player a copy of the same map. Start with an easy one of the local area.

2. Mark your home as the destination, or pick any other place you wish to have the players locate. Mark another place as the starting point—the same for all players.

3. On the word "Go," tell the players to find your starting point on the map. Then, using their felt-tip pens, have them draw the fastest path home. The first player to reach home wins.

4. Be sure to check the route to make sure the player didn't go over any dead ends and other unpassable "short cuts."

5. Play again, this time with a larger, more-detailed map of an unfamiliar area. You may have the players cross the United States to "visit" friends who have moved away to the other side of the nation.

6. Play again, using a map of a foreign country.

7. Award maps or other map-related prizes to the winners.

Variation

Give each player a copy of the same map, and mark the same destination on each one. Have each player mark a starting point. Then have them exchange maps and try to find the routes from the marked starting point to the marked destination.

Barney Darts

We hate him! He hates us! Let's all turn his butt to dust! Play a game of Barney Darts, or make up your own target—Newt Gingrich, perhaps?

Materials Needed
- Large poster of Barney, an unpopular public figure, an old lover, an envied movie star, or an enemy
- Large sheets of corrugated cardboard
- Glue or tape
- Darts, toy guns with rubber suction tips, gooey plastic slime, or other tossable items that will stick

Playing Time: 20–30 minutes

How to Play

1. Glue or tape the poster onto cardboard. Hang the poster on a cardboard-protected wall. Use as many layers of cardboard as you need to protect the wall from darts and dirt, and cover as big a space as you want, to allow for players with bad aim.

2. Offer each player a dart or other item to throw at the target.

3. Have players stand back at a fair distance and take turns throwing the dart at Barney's heart, mouth, brain, or any other location you prefer. Use your imagination if you're aiming at your ex.

4. Award a prize to the player who comes closest to the marked target.

5. Play as many rounds as you like, choosing different targets each time.

Variation
Instead of using a poster of a person, select a picture of a place, such as an unfriendly city, an unpleasant vacation spot, your ex's house, your old reform school, or your former prison.

Beauty Aids

Here's a game for couples to enjoy at a wedding or baby shower. Or play the game any time you feel the need for a makeover!

Materials Needed

- Variety of makeup items, including eyebrow pencils, eye shadow, eye liners, mascara, foundations, highlighters, blush, lip liners, lip gloss, nail polish, nail decorations, and so on
- Variety of makeup applicators and tools—the more obscure and unusual-looking the better—such as cotton swabs, eyelash curlers, tweezers, smudgers, and so on
- Large mirrors
- Towels

Playing Time: 30–45 minutes

How to Play

1. Set makeup materials and mirrors on a large table.

2. Have each player choose a partner of the opposite sex, and have each couple sit next to each other at the table.

3. Tell one male player to choose a makeup item from the collection, say what it is, describe its use, and demonstrate it on his female partner. Then have him pass the item to the next player to use the same way.

4. After the makeup item goes around the table, have the next male player choose another makeup item from the selection on the table, name it, describe it, use it, then pass it on.

5. After all the makeup has been used, let the made-up females look in the mirror. Award a prize for the best makeover.

Variation

Reverse the couples, and have the women make up the men. Or provide the men with a variety of hair-care products, and have them do hair styles instead of makeup. No scissors!

Bedtime Story

Rip open your bodices, use your throbbing imaginations, and create your own group romance novel, one steamy line at a time.

Materials Needed
• Index cards
• Pen or pencil
• Cassette recorder and blank tape
• Romance novels with lusty covers (optional)

Playing Time: 30 minutes

How to Play

1. Set out romance novels to add to the atmosphere. Or, enlarge the covers at a photocopy store, and hang them on the walls.

2. On the index cards, write words commonly found in romance novels, such as hot, steamy, lusty, passionate, throbbing, enormous, silken, quivering, ample, heaving, thrusting, moist, and so on.

3. Shuffle the cards and place them facedown in a pile.

4. Place the blank tape into the cassette recorder, and set the recorder in the center of the room. Attach a microphone, if you have one.

5. Have the first player select the top index card and begin the romance novel, using that word in the first sentence.

6. Tape-record the line as the player speaks.

7. Continue having the players pick cards and use the words in consecutive lines, as the romance novel unfolds.

8. When the last player has wrapped up the story, play the tape back to enjoy the completed masterpiece.

Variation

Instead of writing romance novel words on the cards, have everyone write down humorous or unusual words to be used in a story. If you like, give the players a theme, such as mystery, science fiction, or any other category.

Believe It or Don't

How can you tell when someone is lying or telling the truth? Well, sometimes it's pretty darn difficult!

Materials Needed

- Index cards, 1 for each player
- Pen or pencil

Playing Time: 30 minutes

How to Play

1. Write the word "truth" on one card and the word "lie" on the rest of the cards.

2. Shuffle the cards and place them facedown in a pile.

3. Distribute one card to each player. Tell them to look at their cards but not show them to anyone else.

4. The player with the card marked "truth" must tell a wild, embarrassing, or amusing story that happened to them or someone else—but it must be a true story.

5. The rest of the players must make up a wild, embarrassing, or amusing story that is packed full of lies.

6. Give the players a few minutes to think up their stories, true and false. Then go around the circle and have each player tell a story.

7. When all the players are finished, they must guess who told the true story and who told the lies. Have the truth-teller come forward, and see who got the right answer.

8. Collect the cards, shuffle them, hand them out again, and play another round.

Variation

Search newspapers or humor books for funny and/or unbelievable true stories, and write them on index cards. Mix them in with made-up stories, read them for the group, and have them guess which are true.

Best Friends

How well do you know your friends? Find out their secrets in this surprisingly revealing game!

Materials Needed
- Index cards
- Paper
- Pencils, 1 for each player

Playing Time: 30–45 minutes

How to Play

1. Before the game begins, write down a series of personal questions on index cards, such as "How much do you weigh?" "When was the last time you had sex?" "Who's your favorite movie star?" "What food would you refuse to eat?"

2. Put the stack of cards in the middle of the play area.

3. Have the players pair up with other players they think they know very well. If you've invited couples, let them play together.

4. Distribute paper and pencils.

5. Have one player pick a card from the pile and read the question.

6. Tell each couple that one of them must write down the answer, but keep it hidden from the rest of the players.

7. Go around the room and ask the other players to guess their partners' answers out loud. After each guess, have the players hold up their answers to see if they match. If so, the couple gets a point.

8. Continue playing, taking turns between the two players in each couple, so everyone has plenty of chances to demonstrate how well they know their partner. When everyone has had enough, count the points and award a prize to the couple with the most points.

Variation

Have one player select a card, read the question, and have all the players write down an answer. Then have the player guess everyone's answers, one at a time.

Bet the Lottery

Host your own lottery party, and send your guests home with all kinds of prizes—and surprises!

Materials Needed

- 1 good prize from each player, such as movie tickets, bottle of wine, best-selling book, art print, coffee grinder, and so on (all within a set price)
- 1 booby prize from each player, such as a pair of cartoon-character underwear, funny hat, CD of Milli Vanilli, trash can, and so on (all within a set price)
- Carnival-type tickets or homemade lottery tickets
- Paper
- Pencils, 1 for each player

Playing Time: 30 minutes

How to Play

1. Ask each player to bring one nice prize and one booby prize to the party. Be sure to set a price range, so the gifts are equal in value.

2. Buy or make lottery tickets, two for each player.

3. When your guests arrive, collect prizes in exchange for lottery tickets, paper, and pencils.

4. Have the players write their ticket numbers down on paper. Collect the tickets and put them in a bowl.

6. Select one good prize and display it for everyone to see.

7. Select one ticket from the bowl and read the numbers suspensefully. (Have a drum roll, if you like.)

8. Award the prize to the person holding the matching number.

9. Continue until all the prizes are gone.

Variation

Number the tickets to match the number of prizes. When all the prizes have arrived, assign each one a number. Have the players draw tickets and match drawn numbers to prize numbers.

Birth Write

This is a great game for a baby shower, but it's fun any time you want to know how your friends came into the world!

Materials Needed

- Paper
- Pen or pencil

Playing Time: 30 minutes

How to Play

1. Before the party day, call your guests and ask them to prepare a one-page description of their births. Ask them to call their parents for the details if they don't know much more than the usual stork story. Tell them not to put their names on the paper.

2. Collect the birth stories as the guests arrive.

3. Shuffle the papers, and hand one to each player.

4. Ask the first player to read the birth story he or she was given.

5. When the story is finished, the players must try to guess whose birth it was. It's fun to hear who made a dramatic entry, who came out quickly, who was born in the car, who only weighed four pounds, and so on.

Variation

Instead of asking guests to bring their birth stories, ask for their parents' phone numbers. Call the parents and ask for the birth stories, then read them at the party, and see if each player can identify his or her own birth.

Blinders

Let your fingers do the watching—and guessing—with this challenging game.

Materials Needed

- Blindfolds, 1 for each player
- 10 interesting items to feel, such as Jell-O, Slime, flowers, double-sided tape, cotton balls, a gizmo, a wet washcloth, a slice of pizza, a snail, a ball of hair, and so on
- Paper
- Pencils, 1 for each player

Playing Time: 30 minutes

How to Play

1. Place each item into an individual bag.

2. Give a blindfold to each player, and have them cover their eyes.

3. Give the players paper and pencils, and tell them that they will have to write while blindfolded, so each player should place the paper and the pencil somewhere easily accessible. Half the fun is trying to write on the paper without seeing it.

4. Pass the first item around the circle, and have the players feel it. Ask them not to say anything, but to write down what they think it is. Tell them that none of the items will hurt them, but some may surprise them.

5. Repeat with the rest of the items, until all the player have examined all the items.

6. Tell the players to remove the blindfolds. One by one, reveal the items in the bags in the order in which the players wrote them down. Have the players check their lists to confirm the correct answers.

7. Award a prize to the player with the most correct answers.

Variation

Have one player stand in the middle of the room, blindfolded. Have other players come forward, one at a time, and let the blindfolded player feel their faces, then identify the owner of each face by feel alone. Or forget the blindfolds, and simply have the players feel items inside individual bags and try to guess what they are. This way, players get to watch each other's expressions, which are bound to be as interesting as the items in the bags.

Bobbing for Olives

Here's a tongue-twister that should get your whistle wet at the same time.

Materials Needed

- Plastic champagne or other shallow wide-mouthed glasses or bowls, 1 for each player
- Alcoholic or nonalcoholic drinks, such as martinis or sparkling water
- Olives or cherries
- Paper towels or napkins

Playing Time: 30 minutes

How to Play

1. Set the wide-mouthed glasses around the table, one at each seat.

2. Pour drinks into each glass, filling them three-quarters full.

3. Drop one olive or cherry into each glass.

4. On the count of three, tell the players to retrieve the olive or cherry from the glass, using only their tongues. The first player to get the olive or cherry in his or her mouth wins a prize.

5. Clean up spills with paper towels or napkins before playing another round.

Variation

Instead of having all the guests play at the same time, have them play one at a time, so everyone can enjoy watching each player try to retrieve the garnish. Time them to determine the winner. Instead of using one olive or cherry, fill each container with five or six, and have the players retrieve them all, or see who can retrieve the most in a set amount of time.

Body Language

This is a fast-moving game similar to Charades, based on the box game Guesstures.

Materials Needed

- 50 index cards, cut in half
- 2 pencils
- Stopwatch or timer

Playing Time: 45–60 minutes

How to Play

1. Divide the players into two teams.

2. Give each team fifty half-cards and a pencil.

3. Have each team write down words to be acted out, and assign a point value to the words depending on difficulty. Include twenty-five easy, one-point words, such as horse, pizza, and vest; fifteen moderately challenging, two-point words, such as corner, radio, and sloppy; and ten difficult, three-point words, such as abstract, twins, and toll-collector.

4. Tell the two teams to shuffle the cards and exchange them.

5. Have Player 1 from Team 1 draw four to five cards. Player 1 has one minute to act out all the words for his or her own team. Each time a word is guessed, the player moves to the next word, until time is called. Teams get the point value for each card guessed.

6. Alternate teams and players until all the words are gone.

7. Award a prize to the team with the most points.

Variation

Instead of limiting the number of cards to be guessed per minute, have a player from Team 1 act out as many words as possible, without a limit, before one minute is called. Then have Team 2 do the same. Alternate between teams until all the cards are gone.

Build It Up

Test your sense of balance as you stack up a tall tower, but watch out! Will you be the one to make it tumble?

Materials Needed

• A variety of small flat objects that can be piled on top of one another, such as crackers, cheese slices, dominoes, cards, notepads, coasters, paperback books, matchboxes, CDs, stationary, small plastic tubs with lids, plastic or paper plates, junk mail, and so on

Playing Time: 30–45 minutes

How to Play

1. Collect a variety of small flat objects from around the house, as described above, and lay them out on the table.

2. Seat players around the table, within arm's length of the middle.

3. Have Player 1 select one object from the table and place it in the center.

4. Have Player 2 select a different object and place it carefully on top of the first object.

5. Have Player 3 select another object and place it carefully on top of the second object.

6. Continue going around the table until a player finally causes the tower to tumble over.

7. Begin again, with a new player making the first play, and try to make another tower without letting it fall over.

Variation

If you prefer, build the tower out of one type of item, such as crackers or cookies.

Child Development

How well do you know the basics of child-rearing? Would you pass the parenting test? Time for your checkup!

Materials Needed

• Current book on child development
• Index cards
• Paper
• Pencils, 1 for each player

Playing Time: 30–45 minutes

How to Play

1. Find a current book on child development for your source of game questions. Be sure your information is up-to-date. Include such questions as "When should a baby begin solid foods?" "What is the best toy for a baby?" "Can babies see color or just black and white when they are born?" "Why do babies sleep when the vacuum is running?" Choose generally accepted baby facts, not topics that are under debate.

2. Write the questions on index cards and place them in a pile. Write the answers on a separate sheet of paper.

3. Distribute paper and pencils.

4. Have a player draw a card and read the question to the group.

5. Tell all the players to write down an answer to the question. (Encourage the players to write funny answers in addition to the real answers.)

6. Repeat until all the questions have been read and answered. Read the questions again, this time allowing players to answer aloud. Then read the correct answer. Give a point for each correct answer.

7. Award a prize to the player with the most points.

Variation

Play the game using pet-related questions instead of child-related questions.

Civil War

This game works best when played with couples who have been together a long time, but anyone with enough passion can participate.

Materials Needed

- 20 index cards
- Pencils, 1 for each player

Playing Time: 45–60 minutes

How to Play

1. Divide the players into two teams, preferably men versus women.

2. Give each team ten index cards, and have them write down a point of contention between the sexes. For example, the men might write, "Women should take out the garbage, not men." The women might write, "Men should put the toilet seat down as a common courtesy."

3. Have the two teams sit opposite each other.

4. Shuffle Team 1's cards and place them in a pile. Do the same for Team 2's cards.

5. Have Player 1 from Team 1 pick a card from Team 2's pile and read the topic aloud. That player gets thirty seconds to argue his or her side.

7. When Player 1 is finished, have the group rate the argument on a scale of one to ten, ten being a good argument, one being poor. If the majority agrees that the argument was good, Player 1 gets a point.

8. Continue until every player has had a turn. Make up new topics if you don't have enough, or use the topics more than once.

9. Award a prize to the player with the most points. If there is a tie, have the tying players argue a point against each other, and have the group award points for the best argument.

Variation

Read the topic question, and have everyone write a short argument for or against it. Then have them all read their statements, and vote for the best defense. Or divide the teams based on age or political beliefs.

Classification

Keep those pencils moving if you want to win Classification. Don't stop until you've filled in all the blanks!

Materials Needed

- 13 index cards, cut in half
- Paper
- Pencils, 1 for each player
- Stopwatch or timer

Playing Time: 30–45 minutes

How to Play

1. Write a letter of the alphabet on each index-card half, from A to Z. Shuffle the cards and place them in a pile.

2. Distribute paper and pencils.

3. Ask players to think of eight categories—such as clothing, desserts, animals, presidents, singers, cartoons, road signs, and movies. Tell the players to write the categories down the left-hand side of their sheet of paper (everyone writes the same categories).

4. Have one player draw five alphabet letters from the pile and turn them face up. Tell all the players to write the letters across the top of their papers.

5. Set the timer for two minutes. The players must fill in items for each category that begin with the selected letters—five items for each category, corresponding to the five letters. If the first category is clothing and the first letter is *d,* the player might write "dress."

6. Continue until all the spaces are filled or the timer runs out.

7. When time is up, have the players read their items under each category. If one player's item matches another player's, both must cross off their answers.

8. Award a prize to the player with the most remaining answers.

Variation

Play the game verbally: Pick a category, draw an alphabet card from the pile, and have everyone call out an answer. Players who call out matching answers do not get any points. A player gets a point only if he or she calls out an answer that nobody else matches. When the cards run out, the player with the most points wins.

Claymation

Play this Charades-based game, and everyone will be putty in your hands.

Materials Needed

- Play-doh or modeling clay
- 40 index cards
- 2 felt-tip pens
- Stopwatch or timer
- Paper
- Pen or pencil for keeping score

Playing Time: 30–45 minutes

How to Play

1. Divide the group into two teams and have them sit on opposite sides of a table.

2. Give each group twenty index cards and a felt-tip pen. On each card, have them write down a noun for something that can be shaped in clay, such as cat, table, bus, and so on.

3. Stack the cards in two separate piles. Give Team 1 the pile written by Team 2 and vice versa.

4. Give each group a large lump of clay.

5. Have a player from Team 1 draw a card written by Team 2. That player must create the selected word out of clay and have his or her teammates guess the item before one minute is called. Award a point if the word is guessed correctly.

6. Alternate teams and players until the cards are gone.

7. Award a prize to the team with the most points.

Variation

Instead of restricting the game to nouns, make it more challenging by allowing verbs to be included. Then, if you like, add people, short phrases, movie titles, and so on.

Cliffhanger

Who needs Stephen King? Create your own suspense story, and keep the listeners on the edge of their seats.

Materials Needed

• Flashlight

Playing Time: 30 minutes

How to Play

1. Dim the lights in the party room.

2. Choose one player to begin, and give that player the flashlight. Have the player shine it under his or her chin and begin a suspenseful story.

3. Just as the most exciting part is about to happen—the cliffhanger—have the storyteller pass the flashlight to another player, who must continue the story from that point.

4. Tell the next player to also end at a suspenseful part and pass along the flashlight.

5. Continue until all players have had a turn.

6. Have the last player end the story. The conclusion can be happy or tragic, depending on your group.

Variation

Pick words from the dictionary that suggest suspense, such as screamed, buried, frozen, plummeted, vicious, invisible, bloody, and so on. Write them on index cards, pass them out to players, and have the players include the selected words in the story.

Close-Up

You see your friends all the time, but do you really look at them? Take a closer look with a game of Close-Up.

Materials Needed

• Polaroid camera
• Construction paper
• Cellophane tape
• Paper
• Pencils, 1 for each player

Playing Time: 30 minutes

How to Play

1. As your guests arrive, pull them aside one at a time and take a close-up picture of each of them. You may get a close-up of a pair of lips, a head of hair, a bare foot, a bellybutton, or even a pair of buns.

2. Tape each picture onto a sheet of construction paper. Be sure you note who's who on a separate sheet of paper, in case you forget.

3. Gather the players in a circle, and hold up the first snapshot; then pass it around so the players can take a close-up look.

4. Distribute paper and pencils, and have each player write down who they think the person in the picture is.

5. When all the pictures have been passed around, hold them up again, one at a time, and have the player who matches the picture identify him or herself. Give a point for each correct guess.

6. Award a prize to the player with the most points.

Variation

Take a snapshot of the same body part of each player. For example, take pictures of everyone's hair, lips, or buns. Then pass the pictures around for identification.

Clueless

One by one, gather the clues until you guess who is who. Unless, of course, you're clueless.

Materials Needed
- Paper
- Pencils, 1 for each player

Playing Time: 30–45 minutes

How to Play

1. Distribute paper and pencils, and have each player write down a name of a famous person, keeping it hidden from the other players.

2. Underneath the name, have each player write six clues to the identity of the person, beginning with obscure clues and ending with more obvious clues. For example, if you chose Bill Clinton, you may write, "He played his instrument on *Letterman*," "He doesn't like white-water rafting," "He only pretends to smoke," "He prefers high-flying haircuts," and so on.

3. Have Player 1 begin by reading the first clue on his or her paper. Anyone who thinks they know who the person is may guess. If correct, they get six points for guessing the person's identity on the first clue. If they guess it on the next clue, they get five points, and so on until all the clues are read.

4. Award a prize to the player with the most points.

Variation

Instead of using famous people, play the game using things, places, or events.

Comic Connection

Play a funny game based on the funny papers, and have a few laughs with the gang.

Materials Needed

- Color comic strips from the funny pages
- Felt-tip pen
- Envelopes
- Paper

Playing Time: 30–45 minutes

How to Play

1. Cut out a variety of comic strips from the funny pages.

2. On the back of each strip, draw a wavy line from one end to the other.

3. Cut each strip into individual squares.

4. Mix up the panels of one strip and place them in an envelope. Repeat for the rest of the strips.

5. Divide players into pairs or teams, and give each team an envelope and a sheet of paper.

6. On the word "Go" tell players to remove the comic strip from the envelope and assemble it in the correct order on the sheet of paper. The first team to complete the comic strip correctly wins the round.

7. To make sure the strip is in the correct order, turn it over and see if the wavy line connects.

8. Put the strips back in their envelopes, have the players exchange them, and play another round.

Variation

Mix up all the comic panels and have each player race to find all the same comic strip panels, then put them in order. Or, cut up the same comic strip from different Sundays. Give each player a panel and have them find the other players with panels from the same strip and the same week.

Commercial Quotient

If your guests watch too much TV, they'll be great at figuring out their Commercial Quotient!

Materials Needed

• Cassette recorder and blank tape
• Paper
• Pencils, 1 for each player

Playing Time: 30–45 minutes

How to Play

1. Turn on the television and tape-record a few seconds of popular commercials. *Do not* tape the product name. Leave a few seconds of blank tape between the commercials.

2. As you record the commercials, write down the names of the products on a sheet of paper.

3. At game time, gather the players in a circle around the cassette player, and distribute paper and pencils.

4. Play the tape. Ask players to listen to the commercial jingles and to write down the names of the products.

5. When the tape is finished, play it back and identify each commercial product. Give a point for each product identified correctly.

6. Award a prize to the player with the most points.

Variation

Instead of having the players use paper and pencil to write down their answers, have them race for the answers aloud, to make the game more exciting. Or play TV Quotient by tape-recording theme songs from TV shows and having the players identify the shows.

Common Ground

What do players, pencils, and paper have in common? They all add up to a fun game of Common Ground!

Materials Needed

- 4 or 5 sets of 3 related items
- Paper bags
- Paper
- Pencils, 1 for each player

Playing Time: 30–45 minutes

How to Play

1. Select three common items that have some kind of connection. They can be categorized as person (for example: romance book cover, hairbrush, Italian dictionary—Fabio), place (for example: pineapple, flower, suntan lotion—Hawaii), or event (for example, plastic ants, sandwich, Frisbee—picnic).

2. Place each set of related items into an individual bag.

3. At game time, open one bag, remove one item, and hold it up for all to see. Have the players write down to what this item might be connected. If you like, tell the players to which category each set of items belongs.

4. Remove a second item from the same bag and show it to the group. Tell them they can make a new guess or keep the first guess.

5. Reveal the last item in the bag. Players can make a third guess or keep any of the previous guesses.

6. Announce the connection between the three items. Each player who guessed it right on the first try gets three points. Each player who guessed it right on the second try gets two points. Each player who guessed it right on the third try gets one point.

7. Repeat for the other groups of items.

8. Award a prize to the player with the most points.

Variation

Instead of having the items on hand, list them on a sheet of paper, and read them aloud, one at a time.

Couch Potato

Invite your favorite couch potatoes over for a low-impact game of channel-surfing!

Materials Needed

- TV and remote control
- Paper
- Pencils, 1 for each player

Playing Time: 45–60 minutes

How to Play

1. Gather the couch potatoes around the TV so everyone can see the screen.

2. Distribute paper and pencils.

3. Ask the players to write down ten items they are likely to see on television. Decide whether the items can be generic, such as "potato chips," or specific, such as "Granny Goose potato chips," then have everyone play the same way.

4. When all players have ten items on their lists, turn on the television and give one player the remote control.

5. Have the remote controller begin changing channels slowly, pausing five to ten seconds on each channel.

6. As the players watch the screen carefully, they must try to spot something on their lists. If a player sees an item, he or she should check it off and continue playing.

7. Each time an item is found, the remote control moves to the next player, so everyone gets a chance to flip the channels.

8. Award a prize to the player who finds all ten items first.

Variation

Instead of looking for items, listen for selected words as you flip through the channels.

Could Be Worse

Ever had a day when the washer broke, the dinner burned, the IRS called, and the cat died? Could it be worse? Ask your friends!

Materials Needed

- Paper
- Pencils, 1 for each player

Playing Time: 30–45 minutes

How to Play

1. Have the players sit in a circle; give them paper and pencils.

2. Ask the players to write down an experience when everything seemed to go wrong.

3. Have one player read a bad experience aloud.

4. Have the next player try to top the story with another bad—maybe even worse—experience.

5. Go around the room until everyone has shared an anecdote about a bad time.

6. Have the players rate the bad experiences, beginning with the simply bad, moving to worse, and ending with the very worst.

7. Award a prize to the player with the worst experience.

Variation

Have two players compete for the "worst" title, but this time, one player should lie. Determine who will lie by having the players choose between two face-down playing cards. The player who draws a red card (hearts or diamonds) tells the truth. The player who draws a black card (spades or clubs) must lie. *(Note:* Be sure that only the two players know who is doing what. Keep the cards hidden from the rest of the group.) Have Player 1 relate a bad experience; then have Player 2 try to top Player 1. The group determines who is telling the truth and who is lying.

Creepy Quotes

Even those who are pure in heart and say their prayers at night, will lock all doors, and windows, too, after this game of fun and fright!

Materials Needed

- Memorable quotes from old horror films
- Paper
- Pencils, 1 for each player

Playing Time: 30 minutes

How to Play

1. Before the game begins, write down as many quotes as you can from old horror movies. You can rent classic videos, research the films in library books, or catch them on late-night television several weeks ahead of time. For example: "It's alive!" *(Frankenstein)*, "You'll just be staying the one night?" *(Psycho)*, "Heeerree's Johnny!" *(The Shining)*, "Wake up! They get you when you sleep!" *(Invasion of the Body Snatchers)*, "Michael! Out of the water—NOW!" *(Jaws)*.

2. At game time, distribute paper and pencils.

3. Read the quotes aloud, one at a time, and have the players write down the name of the film and of the character (or actor) who is speaking.

4. Read the questions again, and reveal the answers. Give a point for each correct answer.

5. Award a prize to the player with the most points.

Variation

Ask each player to come to the party with two or three quotes from his or her favorite horror films to share during the game. Or, instead of using quotes from horror movies, try musicals, comedies, action films, or other genres.

Dance Fads

Remember the Twist, the Mashed Potato, the Swim, and the Madison? Play an elimination dance game using all the old steps.

Materials Needed

• Dance music from the forties to the eighties (available on greatest hits collections at a music store)
• Cassette or CD player
• Dance floor

Playing Time: 45 minutes

How to Play

1. Start with the most recent music selected, such as the eighties, and have couples (or singles) dance the first announced dance, such as the Slam or the Bump. Everyone who knows the dance (or can fake it well enough) remains in the game.

2. After a few minutes, change the tune and announce the next dance, such as the Fish or the Walk.

3. Tell all the players to dance the announced dance. Anyone who does not know the dance is disqualified and must leave the dance floor.

4. Continue playing until you run out of dances or until only one couple (or single) remains.

Variation

Have a couple demonstrate a dance from the past. Have the rest of the players try to identify the dance by name. (See also "Dance-Your-Pants-Off Contest," page 32, for another variation.)

Dance-Your-Pants-Off Contest

Watch your guests dance with the flow as they try to keep up with the ever-changing music.

Materials Needed

- A variety of music, such as classical, rock, country, macarena, Irish folk, Russian folk, flamenco, zydeco, square dance, waltz, big band, and so on
- Cassette or CD player
- Dance floor

Playing Time: 60 minutes

How to Play

1. Select a variety of dance-appropriate music, such as classical music for the minuet, country music for the Electric Slide, and so on.

2. Play the first musical selection without telling the couples (or singles) what the dance style is. Tell them that after they hear the first few notes, they must begin dancing the appropriate dance.

3. After a few minutes, change the music to another style and have the dancers change their dancing accordingly. Anyone who doesn't do some semblance of the appropriate dance is out.

4. Continue until all the music has been played or until only one or two dancers remain on the dance floor.

5. Award a prize to the most versatile dancer.

Variation

Have a "snowball" dance: Begin with one couple for the first dance, then have them each find a new partner for the next dance, and so on, constantly increasing the number of dancers on the dance floor. Make sure that with each new dance, the dancers adjust the dance style to the music.

Dangers in the Dark

Better keep a supply of bandages handy—this game can be painful if you don't "watch" where you're going.

Materials Needed

- Blindfold
- Obstacles, such as chairs, pillows, cardboard boxes, large stuffed animals, mattresses, and so on, with no sharp edges or corners
- Index cards
- Stopwatch or timer

Playing Time: 30 minutes

How to Play

1. Cover Player 1's eyes with a blindfold.

2. Have the remaining players create an obstacle course in the game room.

3. When the room is booby-trapped, give each player an index card, and have them stand next to or behind an obstacle.

4. Move Player 1 to the starting point, and tell him or her to collect a card from each player in the room.

5. Tell the players to call Player 1 to come and get the index card. Player 1 must follow their voices to find them as quickly as possible, while being careful to avoid the obstacles in the room.

6. After Player 1 has collected all the cards, note the time.

7. Choose the next player to blindfold, while the rest of the players once again rearrange the obstacles. Play again.

8. Repeat for all the players.

9. Award a prize to the player who collects all the cards in the shortest amount of time.

Variation

Have the players holding the cards keep quiet, instead of calling out, to make the game more challenging.

Dating Game

If you liked the TV show *The Dating Game,* you're going to love it up close and personal.

Materials Needed

- 4 chairs
- Sheet
- Index cards
- Blindfold
- Pen or pencil

Playing Time: 45 minutes

How to Play

1. Place three chairs in the center of the room and a fourth with its back to the three. Hang a sheet between the back-facing chairs, for extra secrecy.

2. On index cards, write down some fun questions for contestants to ask their future "dates." For example: "Player 1, how will you lavish your money on me?" or "Player 2, where would you like to lick me?"

3. On index cards, write down player's names and place them in a box.

4. At game time, select one card at random, announce the name, and have that player sit in the isolated chair. Place a blindfold over the player's eyes.

5. Draw three more names, but do not announce them. Show the names to the crowd and have those three "dates" (of the opposite sex) sit quietly in the chairs behind the blindfolded contestant.

6. Remove the contestant's blindfold, and tell him or her not to turn around. Give the contestant questions to ask the dates.

7. Ask the dates to use a disguised voice when answering—they can change the pitch, use an accent, whisper, and so on.

8. When all the questions have been asked, have the contestant choose a date.

9. Bring the dates out, one at a time, to reveal their identities.

Variation

Offer the contestant a selection of dates from both genders, to add to the fun.

De-fun-itions

This game is similar to the dictionary game, but it is played backwards: de fun starts when the de-fun-itions come before the word!

Materials Needed
• Index cards
• Pencil
• Dictionary

Playing Time: 30–45 minutes

How to Play

1. Using the dictionary, or your own vocabulary skills, write down definitions of common words. For example: "to steal from, or seize control of, a moving vehicle," which would be the definition for "hijack." Have twenty definitions for groups of nine or less players, and forty definitions for groups of ten or more players.

2. Transfer only the definitions to the index cards.

3. Shuffle the cards and stack them in a pile.

4. Have a player draw a card and read the definition slowly.

5. Tell the rest of the players to guess the word and to call it out. The player who first guesses the word correctly gets a point and draws the next word.

6. Continue playing until all the cards are gone.

7. Award a prize to the player with the most points.

Variation

Make the game harder by choosing less-common words and more-difficult definitions.

Detective

Set up a baffling mystery and let your guests solve it using their little gray cells. It's elementary!

Materials Needed

- Short mystery puzzles, available at a library or book and game stores
- Props mentioned in the mystery puzzles
- Index cards
- Detective wear, such as Sherlock hats, magnifying glasses, notebooks, pencils, and so on

Playing Time: 30 minutes

How to Play

1. Select a short mystery puzzle.

2. Set up the crime scene using prop ideas from the story.

3. Write down each clue in the story on separate index cards (or write clues on napkins, newspapers, matchbooks, and so on) and hide them in plain sight around the crime scene. If possible, make enough clues so each player will find at least one.

4. Have detective-players enter the party room and study the crime scene.

5. When a detective finds a clue, have him or her read it out loud.

6. Continue until all the clues are found.

7. Have each detective take a turn guessing whodunit, the weapon and/or method, and the motive.

8. Award a prize to the detective who first solves the mystery.

Variation

Divide the group into two teams and have each team create a mystery for the other team to solve.

Diaper Bag

This is a great game for expectant couples, but you can adapt it to any group. Just let their fingers do the guessing.

Materials Needed

- 10 double paper bags (pink and blue, if you prefer)
- 10 baby items, such as a teething ring, diaper, curved spoon, pacifier, bottle, bib, safety pin, baby powder, squeaky toy, booties, and so on
- Stapler or tape
- Felt-tip pen
- Paper
- Pencils, 1 for each player

Playing Time: 30 minutes

How to Play

1. Place a baby item in a double paper bag. Fold the top over, and staple or tape it closed.

2. Repeat for the remaining items, one baby item per double bag.

3. Number the bags from 1 to 10 on the outside with a felt-tip pen.

4. Have the players sit in a circle. Distribute paper and pencils. Tell the players to write numbers from 1 to 10 down the left side of their paper.

5. Pass Bag 1 around the circle, one player at a time, and allow each player to feel the item *through* the bag (not inside!). Ask the players to write next to number 1 on their paper what they think is inside the bag.

6. Repeat with the other nine bags, one at a time.

7. When finished, hold up Bag 1 and ask everyone to read their answers. Open the bag and reveal the contents to see who is correct. Repeat for the rest of the bags.

8. Award a prize to the person with the most correct answers.

Variation

Instead of using baby items, match the items to your party theme. For a cooking party, place kitchen items in the bags. For a mystery party, use mystery items.

Dictionary

You don't have to be a wordsmith to win at Dictionary. You just have to be a good guesser and bluffer.

Materials Needed

• Dictionary
• Paper
• Pencils, 1 for each player

Playing Time: 45–60 minutes

How to Play

1. Distribute paper and pencils.

2. Give the dictionary to Player 1 and ask him or her to find an unusual or not-frequently-used word and read it aloud.

3. If anyone actually knows the true definition, have Player 1 select a new word. (Remind the players that for the game to be fun, everyone must be honest!)

4. Have Player 1 write down a short version of the correct definition on a strip of paper. Tell the rest of the players to create a definition for the same word, making it sound as real as possible, and to write their definitions on strips of paper.

5. When all the players are finished, have Player 1 collect the papers and read them silently, for practice.

6. Tell Player 1 to shuffle the papers and to read the definitions to the group. The rest of the players must try to guess which one is the real definition and write the answer on another sheet of paper.

7. After everyone has chosen an answer, have all the players announce their selections.

8. Finally, tell Player 1 to read the correct definition aloud. Player 1 gets a point for everyone who did *not* guess the correct answer. And each player who fooled another player into guessing their incorrect answer gets a point.

9. Pass the dictionary to the next player and play again.

Variation

Use a Spanish or French dictionary for added fun.

Disembodied

Would you know the hand of that special person no matter where you were? What about in the dark?

Materials Needed

• Chair
• Blindfold

Playing Time: 30 minutes

How to Play

1. Gather the players in a circle around a chair and assign partners. (This game will be more fun if the partners know each other well—or at least are supposed to know each other well!)

2. Select Player 1 to sit in the chair in the middle of the circle.

3. Blindfold Player 1 and explain that he or she must feel every player's hands, one at a time.

4. Have each player reach out to Player 1, one at a time, and allow Player 1 to examine each hand.

5. After Player 1 has felt all the hands, he or she must tell which one was his or her partner's hand.

6. Repeat for each player.

Variation

Have players try to identify all the hands he or she touches. When you're finished with hands, try feet, hair, faces, or other body parts.

Don't Drop It!

Find out who has fumble fingers, and remember not to give them anything precious to hold.

Materials Needed

- 10 awkward items to pass from hand to hand, such as a feather, flypaper or unpeeled contact paper, popcorn kernel, some Slime, caterpillar, toothpick, glass of water, wet "Wet Paint" sign, towering ice-cream cone, handful of popped popcorn, plate of marbles, and so on
- Large inexpensive gardening gloves, 1 pair for each player (or ask the guests to bring gloves, if you prefer)

Playing Time: 30 minutes

How to Play

1. Set up the items to be passed on a table in a row.

2. Have each player put on a pair of roomy garden gloves.

3. Divide the group into two teams and have each team form a line.

4. Have the first players on each team pick up the first item from the table and pass it carefully to the next player in line. If a player drops or spills the item, it must be returned to the table and passed from the beginning again.

5. The team that passes all the items to the end of the line first wins the game.

Variation

Play a second round of the game, this time keeping your eyes closed as you pass each item!

Don't Say It!

This game sounds easy, but that's what makes it so hard, unless you keep your mouth shut. And that's no fun!

Materials Needed
- Large sheet of paper
- Felt-tip pen

Playing Time: 1 hour

How to Play

1. Make a list of common words that people use frequently. For example: and, the, a, not, do, have, thanks, sorry, don't, want.

2. Write the words on a large sheet of paper, and hang the paper on the wall so everyone can see it.

3. Have one player select a word and circle it with a felt-tip pen.

4. On the word "Go," tell players to carry on their conversations as they normally would, but they cannot use the selected word. When someone uses the selected word, that player loses a point.

5. When that happens, cross off that word, and have another player select a new word to avoid.

6. Continue until all the words are used up.

7. Award a prize to the player who lost the fewest points.

Variation

Instead of changing words, *add* a word that cannot be said while still including the previous words. If "and" is the word selected for the first round, and "the" is the word selected for the second round, neither "and" nor "the" can be used in the second round. And so on. The more forbidden words, the more players will forget and use them, and so the shorter each successive round. (See Talk, Talk, Talk, page 150, for another version of this game.)

Do You Hear What I Hear?

We open and close doors, turn on the water faucet, and do hundreds of other things every day that slam, swish, gurgle, and make a whole array of other noises. Most of us take these noises for granted. If you had to, do you think you could identify them when playing for points? Listen up!

Materials Needed

- Cassette recorder and blank tape
- Paper
- Pencils, 1 for each players

Playing Time: 30 minutes

How to Play

1. Using your cassette recorder, go around the house and tape-record common sounds, such as the alarm clock ringing, water running, toilet flushing, toaster popping up, doorbell ringing, busy signal on the phone, front door slamming, teeth brushing, cappuccino machine brewing, blender whirling, electric drill drilling, garage door opening, and so on. Allow a few seconds between each sound on the tape.

2. Distribute paper and pencils.

3. Ask the players to be quiet and listen to the cassette player. Tell them to identify and write down what they think they hear on the tape.

4. When all the sounds have been played, play the tape again. This time have the players call out their answers, and confirm the ones that are correct.

5. Award a prize to the player with the most correct answers.

Variation

Instead of indoor sounds, tape-record outdoor sounds, bits of music, TV shows, people's voices, or any other noises.

Do You See What I See?

Famous people are always easy to recognize, even behind those giant sunglasses. But what happens when all you see is one part of the person?

Materials Needed

- Large magazine pictures of famous people's faces
- Scissors
- Envelopes
- Paper
- Pencils, 1 for each player

Playing Time: 30–45 minutes

How to Play

1. Tear out magazine pictures of famous folk's faces.

2. Cut the picture of the face into thin strips horizontally in this order: (1) hairline, (2) forehead, (3) eyes, (4) nose, (5) mouth, (6) chin, (7) neck.

3. Mix up the parts of one face and place them in an envelope. Repeat for the rest of the faces, placing them in individual envelopes.

4. Gather the players in a circle and place one envelope in the center.

5. Distribute paper and pencils, and have the players write numbers 1 to 7 down the left side of their paper.

6. Have Player 1 draw a strip from the envelope and place it in the center for all to see.

7. Tell all the players to try to identify the famous person from the first strip and write the name on their sheet of paper. If they can't, they should leave the first number blank.

8. Have Player 2 draw another strip from the envelope and place it in position near or next to the first strip. Players should again try to identify the face.

9. When all the strips have been laid out, the identity of the famous person is revealed. Award points to those who were able to identify the famous person before anyone else.

Variation

Have your guests race to name the famous person aloud instead of writing down the answers. Or mix up strips for three or more faces, divide the players into teams, and have the teams race to pick out the strips that belong together.

Draw!

No art talent is required for this game of fast-draw. But a good eye helps when it comes to identifying the picture.

Materials Needed

- Index cards
- 2 pads of white paper
- 2 felt-tip pens
- Stopwatch or timer

Playing Time: 60–90 minutes

How to Play

1. On index cards, write down items for players to draw, such as a corner, ceiling, fingernail, ripcord, oven timer, cardboard box, and so on. (Make the items simple enough for anyone to draw.)

2. Divide the players into two teams.

3. Give each team a pad of paper and a pen.

4. Have one player draw a card, read it, then show it to a player on the other team.

5. On the word "Go," tell both players from each team that they have a minute to draw the object and have their teammates guess it before the other team. (For very simple objects, you may want to reduce the amount of time to thirty seconds.)

6. Give a point to the team that guesses the item first. If the time runs out and no one guesses the word, neither team gets a point.

7. Repeat with the next two players, and so on, until all the items written on the index cards have been drawn.

8. Award a prize to the team with the most points.

Variation

Have each team make up words for the other team, then have the teams take turns drawing the words.

Earthquake

Sometimes just playing an old favorite on a larger scale adds a whole new dimension to the game.

Materials Needed

• Items to stack, such as blocks of wood, pots and pans, books, boxes, and so on

Playing Time: 30 minutes

How to Play

1. Collect a number of stackable items, the bigger, the more fun, and place them around the room.

2. Have Player 1 choose an item and set it in the middle of the room.

3. Have Player 2 select another item and set it carefully on top of the first item.

4. Continue playing until a player stacks an item that causes the whole construction to fall—Earthquake!

5. Play again, with a different sequence of items and players.

Variation

Take any of your favorite games and make them giant-sized. This strategy works well for checkers, Monopoly, bingo, and so on.

Elementary, My Dear Watson

Can your guests deduce the answer from the bag of clues? Watch the light bulbs go on in the dark!

Materials Needed

- 10 paper bags
- 10 sets of 5 items that go together
- Paper
- Pencils, 1 for each player

Playing Time: 30–45 minutes

How to Play

1. Before the game, collect ten sets of five items that go together. You may collect ingredients for a recipe, clothing for a vacation, books on a particular subject, sports accessories, souvenirs from a geographical location, artist's supplies, carpenter tools, and so on.

2. Place five related items in one bag and close the top. Repeat for other items, grouping them and placing them into individual bags.

3. At game time, distribute paper and pencils. Then open one bag and pull out one item. The players must try to guess the theme of the bag and write down their answers.

4. Bring out another item and have the players guess again.

5. Continue until all the items have been removed from the bag. Give a point to the player who got the answer first.

6. Repeat with the remaining bags.

7. Award a prize to the player with the most points.

Variation

Divide the players into two teams. Dump out five bags of items for one team and the other five bags for the other team. Have the teams race to gather five themed groups of five items each.

Epitaph

Who gets to say the last word to go on the tombstone? Why not make it a team effort with this lively game of posthumous poems?

Materials Needed

• Large sheets of gray poster board or paper, 1 for each player
• 2 felt-tip pens (black would be appropriate)

Playing Time: 30–45 minutes

How to Play

1. Cut the gray poster board or paper into tombstone shapes.

2. Divide the group into two teams and move them into separate rooms.

3. Give each team a list of the players on the other team, a tombstone for each name, and a felt-tip pen.

4. Give the teams twenty minutes to create personalized four-line epitaphs for members of the opposing teams and write them on the tombstones. For example, if a player recently got a bad haircut, you may write, "Here Lies Stephen, Gone Away, Tragic End, to a Bad Hair Day!"

5. Gather everyone in one room and have team members take turns reading the epitaphs. They should be good for quite a few laughs.

Variation

Instead of dividing the players into groups, have them sit in a circle, and have Player 1 begin the epitaph by saying "Here lies _____," and fill in a name. Then have the next player say a second line, followed by a third and fourth from Players 3 and 4. This kind of spontaneous improvisation should result in some funny lines.

Exposed

Watch out what you reveal, or you may be overexposed. Show it off one inch at a time.

Materials Needed

- A large poster of a scantily clad movie star
- Index cards
- Tape

Playing Time: 30–45 minutes

How to Play

1. Hang up a large poster of a hunk or a babe with a lot of skin showing.

2. Write trivia questions on index cards, and number them on the other side. Place them in a stack, number-side up.

3. Cover every inch of the poster with index cards, all numbered to correspond to the trivia question numbers.

4. Have one player choose a card from the stack, turn the card over, and read the trivia question. If the player can't answer the trivia question, the card goes back into the stack, and the turn goes to another player. If the player answers the question correctly, he or she removes the matching card from the poster. Once the card has been removed, that player gets to guess who the poster person is.

5. Continue playing until someone guesses the identity of the poster person.

Variation

Instead of using a poster of a movie star, enlarge a picture of one of the guests to poster size.

Eyewitness

Did you see what you thought you saw? Test your short-term memory to see if you'd make a good Eyewitness!

Materials Needed

- A variety of props, such as a colorful handkerchief, a cookie, a glass of liquid, and anything that is required to set the "scene"
- Paper
- Pencils, 1 for each player

Playing Time: 30–45 minutes

How to Play

1. Set the "scene" with various props.

2. Select one player to be the suspect and have the rest of the players mill about the scene. Have the suspect move through the room for one minute, doing a variety of tasks. For example, the suspect could remove a colorful handkerchief from his or her neck, set it down, take a bite of a cookie, shake hands with someone using the wrong hand, scratch an arm, start to take a drink but stop, set the glass on a different table, say something like "It's hot in here," rub an eye, pat someone on the head, and leave.

3. After the suspect leaves, hand out paper and pencils and ask the players to write down answers to questions about the scene and the suspect. For example: "What color was the handkerchief?" "Where did the suspect put it?" "What did the suspect eat?" "How many bites did the suspect take?" "Which hand was used to shake hands?" "How much did the suspect drink?" "Where did the glass come from?" "What did the suspect say?" "What did the suspect do next?" and "Whom did the suspect pat?"

4. When the players have answered all the questions, reenact the scene, and have them check off what they got right and wrong.

Variation

Instead of asking questions, just have the players write down everything they can remember about the scene.

Famous Movie and TV Quotes

"Are we having fun yet?" Find out with this nostalgic game of famous movie and TV-show quotes.

Materials Needed

- Paper
- Pen or pencil
- Book of famous movie quotes

Playing Time: 45 minutes

How to Play

1. Before game time, collect a list of movie or TV quotes, using books from the library or videos as sources. You may include quotes from such movies as *Ace Ventura: Pet Detective* ("Well, all righty then."), *Psycho* ("You'll just be staying the one night?") *Young Frankenstein* ("Could be worse. Could be raining.") *Star Wars* ("May the force be with you."), *Airplane* ("Don't call me Shirley!"), and so on.

2. Write the quotes on a sheet of paper, and include the speaker and the film or show. For example: "Frankly, my dear, I don't give a damn!" Rhett Butler, *Gone with the Wind.*

3. Gather the players in a circle and tell them you're going to read a quote from a movie or TV show. They must race to call out the name of the movie or show and the character or actor who said the quote.

4. Give a point to the player who says the correct answer first.

5. Continue reading the quotes until all are read.

6. Award a prize, such as a video, to the player with the most points.

Variation

Instead of racing for the answer, have the players write down their guesses. Or, instead of providing quotes, have the players take turns reciting their favorite quotes while the rest of the players try to guess.

Fashion Designer

Find out if your friends are fashion statements or fashion victims. Don't forget to keep the camera handy for embarrassing pictures!

Materials Needed

• Sheets of crepe paper in a variety of colors
• Scissors, 1 or more for each team
• Tape, 1 or more for each team
• Large pair of tights and a T-shirt, for models (optional)

Playing Time: 30 minutes

How to Play

1. Divide the group into teams of four to six players.

2. Have each team select a "model," or draw names to appoint the "dresser's dummy." If you like, have the models change into tights and T-shirts before beginning the game.

3. Provide each team with lots of crepe paper, one or more pairs of scissors, and tape.

4. On the word "Go," give teams twenty minutes to dress the model in a new fashion outfit, using the crepe paper. Encourage them to be elaborate, creative, and unique—the wilder, the better.

5. Tell the teams to stop when you call time.

6. Have the models walk the "runway" to show off their new fashions.

7. Award a prize for the Best Dressed. If you like, award prizes in other categories, such as most creative, most bizarre, sexiest, trashiest, and so on.

Variation

Give the teams creative direction: On strips on paper, write down a number of specific types of fashion, such as ball gown, bathing suit, wedding dress, Halloween costume, and so on. Have each team draw a strip to determine what type of outfit to create.

Fast Word

You'll be a bundle of nerves by the time you finish playing Fast Word!

Materials Needed

- 100 index cards
- Pen or pencil
- Stopwatch or timer

Playing Time: 30–45 minutes

How to Play

1. On index cards, write 100 nouns or verbs that can be acted out, such as stop, toy, rise, elevator, rest, cushion, and so on. Write one word per card.

2. Place the cards in a pile in the center of the room.

3. Divide the players into two teams and have them sit on either side of the card pile.

4. Tell Player 1 from Team 1 that he or she has one minute to draw a card from the pile, act it out, and try to get his or her teammates to guess the word. Until the word is guessed, Player 1 can't go on to the next word.

5. As each word is guessed, have Player 1 continue drawing cards and acting out the words until the minute is up.

6. When time is called, count how many words Team 1 guessed.

7. Then give Player 1 from Team 2 a minute to draw a card and act out the word for Team 2 to guess.

8. Continue alternating players at one-minute intervals until all the cards are used up.

9. Award a prize to the team that guessed the most items correctly.

Variation

If a player gets stuck on a word, allow him or her to pass that word and go to the next word. Subtract a point for each word passed.

Film School

Make your own obscure art films and let the viewers try to guess the message.

Materials Needed

• Video cameras, brought by guests

Playing Time: 2–3 hours

How to Play

1. Ask your guests to bring their video cameras, if they have them.

2. Divide the group into small teams, making sure each team has a video camera.

3. Send the teams out on a videotaping excursion. Tell them to videotape ten items that fit into a theme, such as "the park," which may include close-ups of a flower, an insect, a no-littering sign, bare feet, a Frisbee, and so on, as long as it looks unusual on tape.

4. At an appointed time, have the videotapers return to the game room with their cameras and videotape.

5. Play one of the tapes on the VCR, and have all players try to guess the ten videotaped items, shouting the answers aloud as the items come into view.

6. When the tape is finished, guess the theme.

7. Play the other tapes, and guess the items and themes.

8. Award "Oscars" for a number of categories, such as shortest, most obscure, funniest, weirdest, most annoying, most disgusting, and so on.

Variation

Give each team a theme a few days before the party, and have them videotape items that fit into that theme and bring the tape to the party.

Final Exam

Send your guests back to high school, and find out whether they could pass that history, science, or English test today.

Materials Needed

- High-school textbooks on such subjects as science, math, English, and history
- Paper
- Pencils, 1 for each player

Playing Time: 45 minutes

How to Play

1. Skim through the high-school textbooks, and jot down questions about academic topics. For example: "What is a dangling participle?" "Who was King Richard III?" "What is the purpose of a pancreas?" "What does $E=mc^2$ mean?" "How do you find the diameter of a sphere?"

2. Distribute paper and pencils and announce a "pop quiz."

3. Read the questions aloud, and have the players write down their answers.

4. Read the questions a second time, and have the players read their answers aloud.

5. Read the answers and see which players are correct. Give a point for each correct answer.

6. Award a prize to the player who learned the most in high school.

Variation

Use a spelling bee format: Have players stand and answer questions one at a time. If a player misses the correct answer, he or she must sit down while the others continue. Play until only one player remains standing.

First Time

The "first time" is always memorable, so conjure up those memories and see if you can top your friends!

Materials Needed

• Index cards, numbered for each player
• Paper
• Pencils, 1 for each player

Playing Time: 30–45 minutes

How to Play

1. Seat players in a circle.

2. Have players draw numbered index cards to determine who goes first.

3. Tell the player who draws the index card with the number 1 to begin the game by sharing the details of the first time he or she had sex.

4. Have Player 2 follow by sharing his or her first time, trying to top Player 1's story.

5. Continue until everyone has shared their first times.

6. Have players vote to determine who had the best first time.

Variation

Instead of sharing first-time experiences, write a different question on each index card, such as "Where did you meet your partner?" "Where did you get your first kiss?" "Where was the most outrageous place you had sex?" "What's your favorite body part of the opposite sex and why?" "What was your youngest sexual experience, and how old were you?" "What's one place you'd like to have sex that you haven't yet, and why?" "How many partners have you had and can you name them all?" and "What's one thing you haven't tried that you'd like to?"

Follow Your Nose

This game stinks. But one person's perfume is another person's allergic reaction. Time to sniff a whiff, and try to tell the smell!

Materials Needed

• Variety of popular and identifiable items to smell, such as well-known perfume, pungent beer or wine, best-selling bar of soap, can of baby powder, scented fabric softener, toothpaste, strong cheese, cut-open candy bar, cooking spice, stick of incense, massage oil, air freshener, milk that's gone bad, and so on
• Paper
• Pencils, 1 for each player

Playing Time: 30 minutes

How to Play

1. Put each "smelly" item in a separate container, and cover the containers so players can smell but not see the items.

2. Distribute paper and pencils.

3. Seat the players in a circle, and pass the first item around, allowing each player to take a whiff.

4. Have the players write down what they think they are smelling.

5. When everyone has smelled all the items, reveal the contents and have the players check their answers. Give a point for each correct answer.

6. Award a prize to the player with the most points—something fragrant, of course.

Variation

Add an extra dimension to the game by deducting points from players who show any kind of reaction to the smells.

Food Frenzy

Cook up an evening of fun by creating crazy edible combinations with surprise ingredients. The prize? You get to eat the game!

Materials Needed

- Recipe book
- Ingredients necessary to make a meal (For a breakfast extravaganza, include eggs, onions, green peppers, cheese, bacon, sausage, pancake batter, waffle mix, blueberries, strawberries, potatoes, and so on. For a Mexican dinner, include tortillas, ground beef, refried beans, seasonings, cheese, tomatoes, olives, lettuce, chilies, sour cream, avocados, salsa, and so on.)
- Index cards
- Miscellaneous cooking equipment and ingredients, such as mixer, spoon, oil, salt, and so on

Playing Time: 1–2 hours

How to Play

1. Purchase ingredients necessary to create a particular meal; place them on your kitchen counter.

2. On individual index cards, write down each ingredient.

3. Shuffle the cards and stack them in a pile.

4. Divide the players into two teams.

5. Have the players take turns drawing cards. Each player reads the card and takes the listed ingredient.

6. When all the ingredients have been distributed, give the teams thirty minutes to prepare a dish using the ingredients accumulated by the individual players.

7. When dishes are complete, have players taste (and eat) the results, then vote on the best-tasting dish.

Variation

Give both teams the same ingredients, and see what different dishes they create.

Foreign Phrases

If you're stuck in a foreign country without your phrase book, would you be able to guess what everyone is saying? Finden ze out!

Materials Needed

• Foreign phrase books from a variety of different countries
• Paper
• Pencils, 1 for each player

Playing Time: 30 minutes

How to Play

1. Using several foreign traveler phrase books, write down common expressions in different languages, such as German, French, Spanish, Italian, and Serbo-Croatian.

2. When selecting the phrases, choose the ones that give some clue to the meaning. For example, see if you can translate these German phrases that have similar words in English: *"Es kommt kein warmes Wasser."* ("There's no warm water.") *"Darf ich Sie nach Hause bringen?"* ("May I take you home?").

3. Distribute paper and pencils, and ask the players to write down a translation of each phrase as it is read. You should get some funny responses.

4. At the end of the game, have all the players take turns reading their translations.

5. Award a prize to the player with the most correct translations.

Variation

Simplify the game, and have the players select among four translations (make some of them funny). Or have the players take turns reading foreign phrases for the rest of players, instead of one player reading them all.

Get-Acquainted Bingo

Get-Acquainted Bingo is a great ice-breaker to help your guests start some interesting conversations.

Materials Needed

- Large index cards, 1 for each player
- Variety of colorful stickers, 8 of the same kind for each player
- Felt-tip pen
- Clear contact paper

Playing Time: 30–45 minutes

How to Play

1. Draw a grid on each card, three squares across by three down.

2. Cover the card with clear contact paper on both sides.

3. Place eight of the same stickers on the back of one card. Repeat with the rest of the cards, using a different set of stickers for each player.

4. In each square on the front of each card, write a question about the other players. For example, if someone is pregnant, you might write "Who's expecting a baby?" Be sure to include a question or more about each guest.

5. Have players ask relevant questions to find the players who match the questions on the cards. They can't ask direct questions, but rather beat around the bush, trying to gather the answers.

6. When a player finds a match, have him or her take a sticker from that person and place it over the answered question.

7. Award a prize to the player who first fills all nine spaces with stickers.

Variation

Instead of questions, write down players' favorites, such as TV shows, books, stores, colors, actors, or musicians.

Grabbit

Add a little jolt to your favorite card games with Grabbit!

Materials Needed

- Deck of playing cards
- Small prizes, such as a box of chocolates, single CD, paperback book, upscale magazine, pen set, bottle of wine, decorative item, deck of cards, pocket calculator, blank book, sticky-note tablet, coffee mug, set of postcards, disposable camera, and so on

Playing Time: 1–2 hours

How to Play

1. Display the small prizes on the game table for everyone to admire.

2. Choose your favorite card game, such as hearts, rummy, bridge, canasta, spoons, and so on.

3. Gather the players around the game table.

4. Remove all but one prize from the center of the table, and set the rest of the prizes aside.

5. Distribute the cards and play your favorite card game. Instead of keeping score, the winner gets to keep the prize on the table.

6. Continue playing the same or different games, replacing the prizes on the table after each game.

Variation

Instead of showing the prizes, disguise them with gift wrap or boxes. Then have the winners choose a box and unwrap it to reveal the prize.

Great Minds Think Alike

You don't need ESP to match wits with your opponents, but it sure would help!

Materials Needed

• Index cards
• Paper
• Pencils, 1 for each player

Playing Time: 45 minutes

How to Play

1. On index cards, write down a number of categories. For example: "something you find at the beach," "something that women like," "something that tastes like chicken," "something that floats in the tub," "something that scares most people," "something you eat at a party," and so on. Shuffle the cards, and stack them in the middle of the room.

2. Divide players into two teams, and have them sit on opposite sides of the room.

3. Distribute paper and pencils.

4. Have a player for Team 1 draw a card and read the first category. Give the players on Team 1 one minute to write down as many items as they can for the chosen category. For example, if the category is "something you find at the beach," players may write sand, shells, beach bums, and so on. Ask them to keep their answers secret.

5. When all team members have written their answers, ask them to reveal their answers. If half or more of the players have similar answers, the team gets a point. If not, they don't get a point.

6. Have Team 2 draw a category and write the answers.

7. Continue playing until you run out of categories.

8. Award a prize to the team with the most points.

Variation

Instead of having the teams take turns, have them both respond to the same category. Award points the same way as above.

Guess Who?

How well do you know your friends? Can you always recognize them just by listening to them? Well, listen up and see if you can tell who's who.

Materials Needed

- Cassette recorder and blank tape
- Paper
- Pencils, 1 for each player

Playing Time: 30 minutes

How to Play

1. As the guests arrive, take them in a back room, one at a time, and tape-record them saying something funny, such as a joke or anecdote. Have them disguise their voices as they speak.

2. Leave a second after the disguised voice, and tape them again. This time have them speak using their natural voices, but only saying one word, such as "hello."

3. Leave a second after the hello, and tape them a third time. Tell them to use their natural voices and say a complete sentence.

4. When all the guests have been recorded, gather all the players and distribute paper and pencils. Play the recorded tape, stopping after the disguised voice, and have the players write down who they think is speaking. Play the second recording and have them guess again. Play the third for a final guess.

5. See who guessed the correct answer on the first try and award five points. Award three points for the second try and one point for the third try.

6. Play the rest of the tape, and continue identifying voices until the tape is finished.

7. Award a prize to the player with the most points.

Variation

To make the game more challenging, instead of recording your guests' voices, record the voices of your guests' friends and family.

Hands Off

A task as easy as brushing your hair or putting on your clothes becomes a challenge when you can't use your hands.

Materials Needed

• Materials necessary for simple manual tasks, such as a hairbrush and ribbons, toothbrush and toothpaste, beer and a glass, makeup and a mirror, child's book, shirt with buttons, shoes and socks, and so on
• Stopwatch or timer

Playing Time: 30 minutes

How to Play

1. Choose a variety of simple tasks that normally involve the use of the hands.

2. Present the players with the items necessary to complete each task; tell them not to touch the items until their turn.

3. Have Player 1 begin by trying to accomplish a task without using his or her hands. If Player 1 is given a brush and a ribbon, that player must brush his or her hair and tie a ribbon in it—all within a limited period of time (one to two minutes).

4. When Player 1's time is up, have Player 2 complete the task indicated by his or her items. And so on, until all players have had a chance to complete their tasks. For example: Player 2 must brush his or her teeth with the toothbrush and toothpaste. Player 3 must pour a can of beer into a glass and drink it. Player 4 must apply some makeup. Player 5 must open a book, then turn a page. Player 6 must put on a shirt and button it (or take it off). Player 7 must put on socks and shoes, then try to tie the laces.

5. When all the tasks are completed, award a prize to the player who was most successful.

Variation

Have the players work in pairs.

Hatfields Vs. McCoys

You think the Hatfields and McCoys were feuding? That was nothing compared to your own personal game of Hatfields vs. McCoys.

Materials Needed

- Series of easy questions based on a favorite theme, such as sports, food, literature, or a combination
- 2 bells
- Paper and pencil to keep score

Playing Time: 60 minutes

How to Play

1. Divide the players into two teams. Name one team the Hatfields and one team the McCoys.

2. Seat the teams on opposite sides of the play area, and place a bell on each side, accessible to all players on the team.

3. Appoint one person as the game show host who reads the questions. The questions should be easy, since this is more of a race for the answer than a game of knowledge.

4. Tell the teams to ring the bell as soon as a question is read.

5. Have the host determine who rang the bell first and ask that team to answer the question. If the answer is correct, the team gets a point. If it's incorrect, the other team gets a chance to answer. If they are correct, they get the point. If no one is correct, move to the next question.

6. Continue until all the questions are asked.

7. Award a prize to the team that won the battle.

Variation

If you're asking only sports questions, name the teams after rivaling sports teams, such as the Cowboys vs. the Braves. If you're asking food questions, name the teams after food experts, such as Julia Child vs. Martha Stewart.

Holiday Trivia

How much do your guests know about the holidays they celebrate? Find out with Holiday Trivia.

Materials Needed

• Index cards
• Pen or pencil
• Books about holidays

Playing Time: 30–45 minutes

How to Play

1. Look through books for holiday trivia. Use the information to write questions. For example, for Christmas you may ask, "What are the names of the eight reindeer?" "Who wrote 'The Night Before Christmas'?" or "What is the definition of Tannenbaum?"

2. Write three to five questions for all the holidays you wish to use, including New Year's Eve, Valentine's Day, Easter, Halloween, Thanksgiving, Hanukkah, and Christmas. Add minor holidays if you like, such as Groundhog Day, Labor Day, Mother's Day, and Boxing Day. Write one question per index card.

3. Shuffle the holiday trivia cards and stack them in a pile. Have players draw a card from the top and answer the question. Give a point for each correct answer.

4. Award a prize to the player with the most points.

Variation

If you're hosting a party on a special holiday, choose trivia questions related only to that holiday. Or read the trivia questions and have the guests race to answer. You can also play this game in teams, or like a spelling bee, with guests dropping out if they miss a correct answer.

How Old Were You Then?

Do your guests remember how old they were when the Cold War ended? The terrible tornado hit? The president threw up?

Materials Needed

- Dates of big past events, such as natural disasters, political assassinations, memorable holidays, trips to the moon, movie star marriages, city riots, sex scandals, and so on
- Paper
- Pencils, 1 for each player

Playing Time: 30–45 minutes

How to Play

1. Using newspapers or magazines at the library as sources, research big events. Record the events and the corresponding dates on an answer sheet. Photocopy the headlines, if possible, blocking out the dates.

2. Gather the players in a circle and distribute paper and pencils.

3. Hold up the first headline or announce the first big event.

4. Tell the players to write down the date of the event, where they were at the time, and how old they were.

5. After the players write the answers to all the announced events, reveal the dates.

6. Have the players read their answers to see who remembered the best. Give a point for each correct answer.

7. Award a prize to the player with the most points.

Variation

Photocopy the headlines, such as "Man Lands on the Moon" and "Fire Burns Down Chicago," and cut them up into two or three sections. Set out all the sections, and have the players try to rearrange the headlines. You should come up with some funny headlines, such as "Fire Burns Down the Moon" and "Man Lands on Chicago."

How to Have a Perfect Marriage

If you think you know everything necessary to have a perfect marriage, share your advice with others and see who agrees.

Materials Needed
• Paper
• Pencils, 1 for each player

Playing Time: 30–45 minutes

How to Play

1. Distribute paper and pencils.

2. Have the players write down one piece of advice they would give a couple planning to get married, or a newlywed couple.

3. When everyone has a piece of advice ready, have one player read his or her advice to the group.

4. Have the rest of the group debate the advice, offering points and counterpoints.

5. When the advice has been thoroughly examined, the group can vote on its merits. If the majority votes for the advice, the advice giver gets a point.

6. Move on to the next piece of advice. Continue playing until everyone has had a chance to offer advice.

7. Award a prize to the player with the most points.

Variation

Instead of marital advice, offer advice on any selected topic, such as getting a job after college, meeting the opposite sex, dating tips, parenting tips, sex tips, and so on.

Hunter/Gatherer

You're not going to feed those freeloading guests by just handing over the food, are you? Make them work for their meals!

Materials Needed

• Finger foods, snacks, appetizers, and other portable edibles
• Drinks in bottles or cans

Playing Time: 30 minutes

How to Play

1. Place all the food and drinks into portable, sealed serving containers. (You don't have to use sealed containers, but hey, it's your carpet and furniture!)

2. Hide all the food and drinks throughout the house—in the bathtub, on top of the refrigerator, in the piano seat, behind the couch, in the cupboards, on the fireplace, in the bedroom, and so on.

3. Set out napkins for the guests, but nothing else.

4. When all the guests have arrived, tell them they're going on a treasure hunt—for the party food.

5. Send the guests in search of their nourishment, and have them bring back what they find to the party table.

Variation

Instead of having the players bring back the food, tell them they can take some of what they find but must leave the rest hidden for other guests to find.

Hyphenated Honeymooners

What if Glenn Close married Sean Penn? She'd be Glenn Penn! Bo Derek and Don Ho? Bo Ho! What about Snoop Doggy Dogg and Winnie the Pooh? I guess those two will never get together!

Materials Needed

• Paper
• Pencils, 1 for each player

Playing Time: 30 minutes

How to Play

1. Distribute paper and pencils.

2. Ask the players to write down the name of a famous female movie star, politician, character, or world figure, such as Yoko Ono, Goldie Hawn, or Whitney Houston.

3. Have them all pass their papers to the right.

4. Then have them pair the person listed on the paper with another famous person to create a new and funny name. (The women can keep or drop their maiden name—whichever way is funniest.) For example, if Yoko Ono married Sonny Bono, she'd be Yoko Ono Bono. If Goldie Hawn married Ron Silver she'd be Goldie Silver. And if Whitney Houston married Gene Pitney, she'd be Whitney Pitney. Hey, if Phyllis Diller married Bruce Willis, divorced him and married Dobie Gillis, divorced him and married Mel Tillis, she'd be Phyllis Willis Gillis Tillis! And if Sondra Locke married Elliott Ness, divorced him and married Herman Munster, she'd be Sondra Locke Ness Munster!

Variation

Instead of having the women change their names to the men's last names, have the men change their names to the women's last names. Or marry couples of the same gender. What if Woody Allen married Natalie Wood, divorced her and married Gregory Peck, divorced him and married Ben Hur? He'd be Woody Wood Peck Hur!

Infamous Last Words

Most people can identify famous books by their first lines, but how many books can they identify after hearing only the last lines?

Materials Needed

- A collection of classic books, available at the library
- Index cards
- Paper
- Pencils, 1 for each player

Playing Time: 30–45 minutes

How to Play

1. Before the party, write down the last lines from a number of famous and/or classic books. You may include adult books, such as *Gone with the Wind, Moby Dick,* and *The Scarlet Letter.* Or use old familiar children's books for a trip down memory lane, such as *Peter Pan, The Wind in the Willows, The Cat in the Hat,* and so on. Write one line per index card.

2. During the party, distribute paper and pencils.

3. Tell the players you are going to read some last lines from famous books and they must write down the name of the book.

4. After you have read all the last lines, share the answers to see who got the most correct.

Variation

To make the game easier, have the players match the lines to a list of book titles.

Information Processing

You don't have to belong to Mensa to win this game. You have a one-in-three chance of guessing the right answer.

Materials Needed

• Encyclopedia
• Index cards
• Felt-tip pen

Playing Time: 1 hour

How to Play

1. Research information tidbits from the encyclopedia.

2. On an index card, write down a question based on the information, and offer three choices for the answer: one correct and two incorrect. For example: The Holstein cow is: (1) brown with spots, (2) all black, or (3) black and white. Create as many of the question cards as you like.

3. Select two players to begin the game, and have them stand at the front of the room.

4. Ask Player 1 a question, and have him or her choose one of the three answers. If Player 1 answers correctly, he or she remains standing. If the answer is wrong, Player 1 sits down, and Player 2 gets a chance to answer the question.

5. If Player 2 answers the question correctly, ask him or her a new question and offer three choices. Player 2 remains in the game if the answer is correct, and must sit down if incorrect.

6. As the players drop out, replace the two in front of the room. Take turns asking and answering questions, so everyone gets a chance to do both. Continue until only one player remains.

Variation

Use questions that have more than one correct answer, or choose questions around one theme.

Ingredients

They say, you are what you eat. But do you really know what you eat?

Materials Needed

- Candy bars, desserts, appetizers, drinks, or other food items with multiple ingredients
- Index cards
- Paper
- Pencils, 1 for each player

Playing Time: 30 minutes

How to Play

1. Gather or prepare a variety of snacks, such as a Snickers, tiramisu, crab puffs, egg cream, or other party food. Be sure they contain several ingredients.

2. Write the ingredients down on individual, numbered index cards. Create an answer sheet with the name and ingredients of the snack next to corresponding number. Stack the cards in a pile.

3. Distribute snacks, paper, and pencils, and ask the players to write down all the ingredients in the snack they received.

4. When the players have finished tasting the snack and writing down the ingredients, read the answer sheet with the ingredients list to see who got the correct answer.

5. Continue nibbling, sipping, and guessing until the food and drinks are gone.

Variation

Have the guests bring their favorite dishes to the party, along with the recipes. Then have the players guess the ingredients in each dish. (The person who brings the dish doesn't get to guess the ingredients in his or her dish!)

Keep Quiet!

How difficult could it be to keep quiet for a short period of time? Find out while the rest of the party goes on gabbing!

Materials Needed

• Stopwatch or timer

Playing Time: 1 hour

How to Play

1. Explain to your guests that one player will be chosen to start the game. That player must try not to talk for a set period, say five minutes.

2. When the game begins, start the timer and signal Player 1 to stop talking.

3. In the meantime, tell the rest of the players to try to get Player 1 to speak, using any method they can.

4. If Player 1 speaks, have him or her select another player to keep quiet and the game continues. If Player 1 keeps quiet for the entire time period, he or she wins a small prize and then selects another player to keep quiet.

5. The game ends when all the players have had a turn keeping quiet.

Variation

Make the game more challenging: Tell the selected player not to talk, laugh, make any facial expressions, or use any kind of body language.

Kiss Me, I'm Irish

You can play this game on St. Patrick's Day or make adaptations to other cultures and play any day of the year.

Materials Needed

- Irish trivia, or trivia about other cultures, countries, and so on
- Paper
- Pencils, 1 for each player

Playing Time: 30–45 minutes

How to Play

1. Research Irish culture, St. Patrick's Day in particular.

2. Write down trivia questions, such as "Who was St. Patrick?" "Why do we wear green on St. Patrick's Day?" "What's the significance of a four-leaf clover?" and so on.

3. Distribute paper and pencils.

4. Read the trivia questions and have the players write down the answers.

5. Read the answers at the end of the game and give a point for each correct answer.

6. Award an appropriate prize, such as Irish beer, chocolate gold coins, or a book on Irish lore, to the player with the most points.

Variation

Make a multicultural game and include questions from other cultures, such as African, Alaskan, Asian, Australian, European, Indian, and so on. Or have your guests bring trivia questions regarding their own culture to share with the group.

Know the One You Love

How well do you know the one you love? This game may be based on TV's *Newlywed Game,* but you don't have to be married to enjoy it.

Materials Needed
• Index cards
• Paper and pencil to keep score

Playing Time: 45 minutes

How to Play

1. Call couples before the party, one person at a time. Make sure their partners are not around when you ask the preselected questions.

2. Ask each player some semipersonal questions, such as "What's your favorite romantic spot?" "Where did you two go on your first date?" "What time do you go to bed at night?" "What do you do the first thing in the morning?" "What was your last fight about?" "What position do you sleep in?" "What turns you on?" and so on.

3. Ask the other half of the couple a different set of questions.

4. Record each question on one side of an index card, and the answer on the other. Keep the cards for each person in separate piles.

5. At game time, ask one half of Couple 1 a question about the other half. Award a point if the response matches the answer on the card. Repeat for each half of the remaining couples.

6. Then ask the other half of all the couples the remaining questions, and award points if they guess their partner's answers.

7. Add up the points to see which couple knows one another best.

Variation
Play this game at a bridal shower with women only. Quiz the bride on how well she knows her groom, and have the groom make a surprise appearance to confirm the answers.

Liar's Club

Can you really trust your friends to always tell the truth? Watch out—they're all a bunch of liars when a game prize is at stake.

Materials Needed
- Index cards
- Pencils, 1 for each player

Playing Time: 30–45 minutes

How to Play

1. Divide the players into two teams and give each team a bowl.

2. Have each player write an embarrassing moment on an index card. Tell them to leave the bottom half of the card blank, and to write their names on the back. Have all players place the cards into their team's bowl.

3. Exchange bowls and have each player draw a name from the other team's bowl.

4. Then, have the players write another embarrassing moment, this time completely made up, on the index cards they drew—under the true embarrassing moment already there.

5. Place all the cards in stacks for each team.

6. Have Player 1 from Team 1 draw a card from Team 2's pile, announce the name on the back, and read both the true and false anecdotes aloud in random order.

7. Tell Team 1 to guess which story is true and which one is a lie. Award points for correct answers.

8. Continue alternating players and teams until all the cards have been read. Add the points to see which team wins.

Variation

Instead of having players read the names on the cards, just read the anecdotes and let them guess who's who. (In this version, you won't need the made-up story, just the real one.)

Liar's Dice

Based on the popular bar game of dice, this version of Liar's Dice will make con artists out of your most honest friends.

Materials Needed

• Dice, 5 for each player
• Dice cups, 1 for each player
• Pennies or candies for betting

Playing Time: 45 minutes

How to Play

1. Give each player five dice and a dice cup.

2. Distribute equal amounts of money or candy for betting.

3. Have each player shake the dice in the cup and roll them out on the table. Everyone's goal is to roll the best hand: (1) five of a kind, (2) four of a kind, (3) full house (three of a kind and a pair), (4) three of a kind, (5) two pair, (6) two of a kind, or (7) the highest number on one die.

4. After the first roll, let each player keep as many dice on the table as he or she wants, in an attempt to collect a good hand. Each player then gets one more turn to try to get a good hand. But this time, the player keeps the results of the second roll hidden beneath the dice cup.

5. After all the players have had their second rolls, have all the players place bets. Since the players don't know what's hidden beneath their own or anyone else's dice cup, they must take a chance with their bets.

6. Once the bets have been made, reveal the hidden dice. The player with the best hand wins the pot.

Variation

Use multicolored dice and add more levels to win, such as flush, full house of the same color, and so on.

Lip-Sync Contest

A little lip-action, and anyone can be Madonna or Prince. But can the newly formed stars convince an audience?

Materials Needed

- Cassette or CD player and popular tapes or CDs
- Lyrics to each song provided
- Stand, for the song lyrics

Playing Time: 30 minutes

How to Play

1. Have guests choose a favorite song from your stack of tapes or CDs.

2. Give them the lyrics to go with the song.

3. At show time, have a player come to the "stage" and lip-sync his or her song along to the music. Provide a stand for the lyrics so the player can read the words.

4. After all performers have completed their acts, vote on the best fake singer.

5. Be sure to videotape the event; replay it for laughs at the end of the live show.

Variation

Divide the players into teams or duets, provide costumes and accessories, and let the teams practice a few times in separate rooms before presenting their acts.

Little-Known Facts

Through deduction and elimination, can you tell which member of the group is "It"? Be on your guard—anyone can be "It," even you!

Materials Needed

• Index cards
• Paper
• Pencils, 1 for each player

Playing Time: 45 minutes

How to Play

1. Before the party, question partners, relatives, or friends, to find out little-known facts about your party guests, such as where they were born, what they were for Halloween, what they wanted for Christmas, where they worked in high school, where they went on vacation, what they do at work, and so on. Write ten facts for each player—one fact per index card—and include the player's name on each card.

2. At game time, distribute paper and pencils.

3. Place the piles of each player's facts (ten per pile) in a row in front of you.

4. Take one card from each pile and shuffle them.

5. Read one of the facts from an index card, and have players write down who they think the person is.

6. After all the facts are read for each player, reveal the answers and see who guessed the most correct.

7. Take one more card from each player's pile, shuffle them, and play again.

8. After the tenth round, award a prize to the player with the most correct answers.

Variation

Select one of the players, then read a list of five facts along with five falsehoods about that person. Have the other players guess which "facts" are true and which are false.

Logic and Deduction

Gather your friends for a battle of wits with a game of Logic and Deduction!

Materials Needed

- Book of mind puzzles and brain teasers
- Index cards
- Paper
- Pencils, 1 for each player

Playing Time: 45–60 minutes

How to Play

1. Check the bookstore or library for a book of brain teasers; select your favorites—visual puzzlers, math problems, logic questions, language tricks, or any other kind of mind puzzle.

2. Write each one down on an index card, along with the solution.

3. Distribute paper and pencils.

4. Have one player select an index card and read the puzzle to the group.

5. Have the rest of the players race to solve the puzzle and call out the answer. If the first called-out answer is correct, the player who called it out gets a point. Then a new player selects another card, reads the puzzle, and has the group solve it. If the first called-out answer is incorrect, players keep guessing until the puzzle is solved.

6. Continue drawing index cards and sharing the puzzles until all are gone.

7. Award a prize to the player with the most points.

Variation

Have the players work in teams instead of individually.

Lost Vowels

We all take vowels for granted. But what if all the vowels were suddenly lost, and only consonants remained?! N YR MRK, GT ST, G!

Materials Needed

• Paper
• Pencils, 1 for each player

Playing Time: 30–45 minutes

How to Play

1. Before the guests arrive, write down twenty popular movie titles, such as *Gone with the Wind, Ben-Hur, Star Wars, Raiders of the Lost Ark, Frankenstein, Independence Day, Babe,* and so on.

2. Go through the list and cross off all the vowels, including the letter *y.*

3. Rewrite the list on a sheet of paper, one movie title on each line—leave out the vowels, and close up the spaces between the letters. Capitalize every letter. For example: GNWTHTHWND, BN-HR, STRWRS, RDRSFTHLSTRK, FRNKNSTN, NDPNDNCD, BB.

4. Photocopy the list for each player.

5. At game time, give each player a copy of the list and a pencil.

6. On the word "Go," have the players race to decipher the movie titles, adding the appropriate vowels and spaces.

7. Award a prize to the first player to complete the list.

Variation

Play again, this time using song titles, names of familiar people, vacation spots, candy bars, restaurants, or any category you like.

Lottery Spin

The odds are better when you set up your own Lottery Spin. How much do you want to bet?

Materials Needed

• Stiff white paper or poster board
• Felt-tip pens

Playing Time: 30 minutes

How to Play

1. Ask the players to bring nickels, quarters, or dollar bills to the party.

2. Cut the paper or poster board into lottery-ticket-sized strips. Number each one. Repeat so that you have two sets of lottery tickets with the same numbers.

3. Determine a price for the tickets, and ask the players how many tickets they want to purchase. For each purchase, give the player a numbered ticket, and place the other ticket with the same number into a bowl.

4. Place all the collected money in a pot.

5. Mix up the tickets in the bowl and select one. The player with the corresponding number wins the pot.

Variation

Make several pots, each larger than the next, and have a number of winners. Or play Keno: Number paper strips from 1 to 100, and place them in a bowl. Have the players write down five numbers from 1 to 100. Draw numbers from the bowl until someone's five numbers are all selected.

Lotto Luck

If you're good at predicting your guests' behavior, this game should bring you a Lotto Luck.

Materials Needed

- 5-by-5-inch poster board squares, 1 for each player
- Pencils, 1 for each player

Playing Time: 2–3 hours

How to Play

1. Draw a grid with five columns and five rows on each poster board square to make lotto cards.

2. Give each player a lotto card and a pencil.

3. Ask the players to fill out each grid square with a prediction for each player to fulfill during the evening. For example, a player may write, "Jack will show us his scar," "Jill will cover her mouth when she laughs," "Tom will say the 'F' word," "Terri will spill her drink," and so on.

4. Tell the players to keep their cards handy, but not visible to other players, and to mark an *x* in the square whenever one of the predictions comes true. The first person to complete his or her lotto card wins the game.

5. If the party ends and no one has completed the card, check to see who has crossed off the most squares.

6. Share the lotto cards with one another to see what other people predicted.

Variation

To make the game easier, if any player gets five across, five down, or five diagonally, he or she wins.

Love Is . . .

Poets are always trying to capture the essence of love in words. Have you got what it takes to make the poets give up their pens?

Materials Needed

- 50 index cards
- Paper
- Pencils, 1 for each player

Playing Time: 30–45 minutes

How to Play

1. Before the game begins, write twenty-five romantic or sexy words on the index cards, such as throbbing, lips, passion, candlelight, steaming, thighs, heaving, chest hair, roses, titillating, hot, and so on.

2. On another twenty-five index cards, write some silly images, such as ironing board, wallpaper paste, motor oil, abs of steel, nose hair, bikini wax, garlic press, and so on.

3. At game time, stack the two piles separately in the center of the party room.

4. Distribute paper and pencils.

5. Have each player draw card from each pile.

6. When everyone has two cards, ask them to write a silly love poem, using the two words or phrases they have drawn. For example: "Roses are red. / They make me *hot*. / Your eyes are sexy. / Your *nose hairs* are not."

7. When all the players have finished their poems, have them read their work aloud to the group, one at a time, for a good laugh.

Variation

Have the players pick two cards from each pile to make the game more challenging. Change the poetic genre, and use mystery words, or some other category, instead of romance words.

Lovers' Connection

Couples are always curious about how other couples met. Who has the most interesting first-meeting story?

Materials Needed

• Paper
• Pencils, 1 for each player

Playing Time: 30 minutes

How to Play

1. Distribute paper and pencils.

2. Have the players jot down a brief sketch about how they met their partners. If some are single, have them write down how they met a particular lover, or make something up.

3. When everyone has finished writing, go around the room and have each player read what they wrote. If some of the players are couples, let them each tell their version of the meeting, and see how similar they are.

4. After all the players have told their stories, vote on the best one. If you like, award prizes for weirdest, most romantic, sleaziest, most unlikely to have happened, and so on.

Variation

Have couples write down their meetings and hand them to the emcee, who reads each story. Then tell the other players to guess who wrote which story.

Lucky Strike

Throwing a ball down an alley to knock down a few pins may be fun, but it's a lot more interesting when the pins are prizes!

Materials Needed

- 12 prizes, wrapped in boxes (At least 3 of them should be booby prizes, such as giant-sized underwear, a tape of the macarena, Mr. Potato Head, and so on—nothing breakable!)
- Masking tape
- Blindfold
- Tennis ball

Playing Time: 30–45 minutes

How to Play

1. Wrap gifts inside small boxes, and set them in a bowling-pin arrangement, spaced a foot apart from one another.

2. Mark two alley lines and a foul line along the floor with masking tape.

3. Have Player 1 step to the foul line. Give him or her a blindfold and a tennis ball.

4. Have Player 1 put on the blindfold and try to roll the ball down the lane. Player 1 may keep any prizes he or she hits.

5. Have the next player take a turn, and so on, until all the prizes are gone.

6. After the game is over, tell the players to open their prizes to see what they won.

Variation

Set up a miniature golf course using prizes as the holes.

Mad Advertising

What do you notice when watching TV commercials—the product name or the trivial details in the background?

Materials Needed

• TV and remote control
• VCR and blank videotape
• Paper
• Pencils, 1 for each player

Playing Time: 30–40 minutes

How to Play

1. Before the party begins, record fifteen to twenty of your favorite commercials. The funny ones are usually the most popular.

2. Watch the tape several times, and write down one obscure question about each commercial, such as "What time did the clock show?" "How many women were in the office?" "What did the man's name badge say?" "What did the kid say to his mother?" "How many times does the dad pull the waffle?" and so on.

3. Gather the players around the TV so everyone can see the screen, and give each player paper and a pencil.

4. Pop in the prerecorded tape and play the first commercial.

5. After the commercial is over, stop the tape with the remote control. Read the question you have written down about that particular commercial, and ask the group to write their answers on their sheets of paper.

6. When everyone has an answer, rewind the commercial and play it again to see who got it right. Move on to the next commercial.

Variation

Offer the players a choice of answers to make the game easier, such as "Did the clock say (a) 10:00, (b) 11:30, or (c) 12:00?"

Memories

You'll have to go back to your childhood to come up with the answers to Memories.

Materials Needed

• Reference books from the forties to the seventies
• Index cards
• Paper
• Pencils, 1 for each player

Playing Time: 30–45 minutes

How to Play

1. Before the day of the party, pick up a reference book about a past era from the library or bookstore. *Time-Life Books* and *When We Were Young,* by Kleinfelder, both contain information on popular foods, toys, games, clothing, music, and other categories.

2. Use the information to create trivia questions. For example: "In which year did The Beatles sing on the *Ed Sullivan Show?*" "What was the last name of Ricardo's neighbors?" "On what show did Gale Storm appear?" "How many years did *Star Trek* run on TV?" "What was a poodle skirt?" "What was the name of the most popular Chevrolet in 1957?" "What are the ingredients in a tuna casserole?" Write one question per index card.

3. At game time, distribute paper and pencils.

4. Read the questions, one at a time, and ask players to write down their answers.

5. When all the questions have been read, repeat the questions and let the group read their answers. Give a point for each correct answer.

6. Award a prize to the player with the most points.

Variation

Concentrate on one category, such as music—past to present.

Mind Match

If you can't keep your mouth shut, play this game of Mind Match, based on the box game Outburst!

Materials Needed

- 40 sheets of paper
- 2 pencils
- Stopwatch or timer

Playing Time: 30–45 minutes

How to Play

1. Think of twenty different categories, such as school subjects, sports cars, comedy shows, brands of cereal, and so on.

2. Write a different category at the top of each sheet of paper, leaving twenty sheets blank.

3. Divide the players into two teams. Give each team ten sheets of the paper with categories, ten blank sheets, and a pencil, and send them to different rooms.

4. Tell the teams to write down ten of the most common examples for each category. For example, if the category is school subjects, the team may list math, science, English, social studies, physical education, history, psychology, art, computers, and business.

5. After both teams have completed their ten categories, have them come together to start the game.

6. Have Team 1 announce one of their ten categories. Team 2 has one minute to write down as many examples as they can in that category.

7. When the minute is up, have Team 2 read their list aloud. They gets a point for every item on their list that matches Team 1's list.

8. Continue alternating teams and players until you go through all the categories.

9. Award a prize to the team with the most points.

Variation

Play the game in couples instead of teams. Before the party begins, prepare ten examples for each category. Pair up players, call out a category, and have each pair try to come up with as many items as they can in one minute. Then read your preselected list to see which couple got the most matches.

Monster Movie Charades

Add a twist to the standard game of Charades by giving it a theme: movie monsters.

Materials Needed

- 40 index cards
- 2 pens
- Stopwatch or timer

Playing Time: 45–60 minutes

How to Play

1. Divide the players into two teams.

2. Give each team twenty index cards and a pen and send them into separate rooms.

3. Ask the teams to write down twenty monster movie villains that the other team must act out, such as Frankenstein's Monster, Swamp Thing, Godzilla, Wolfman, The Blob, Dracula, and so on—one villain per index card.

4. When both teams have completed their list of twenty monsters, have them sit on opposite sides of the party room.

5. Have a player from Team 1 draw a card from Team 2's pile.

6. Using a stopwatch or timer, give Player 1 two minutes to act out the monster for his or her team to guess. If Team 1 guesses correctly within the time frame, they get a point. If not, they get no point.

7. Then have a player from Team 2 draw a card from Team 1's pile and act out the character.

8. Continue alternating teams and players until you go through all the characters.

9. Award a prize to the team with the most points at the end of the game.

Variation

Instead of acting out characters, act out scenes from monster movies for true horror buffs to guess.

Movie Star Trivia

We often know more about movie stars than we do about our own friends. Take this trivia test to discover your star quotient.

Materials Needed

- Books, fan magazines, tabloids, gossip columns, and other sources of star trivia
- Index cards
- Paper
- Pencils, 1 for each player

Playing Time: 30–45 minutes

How to Play

1. Before the day of the party, gather trivia questions about famous stars (use the library as a resource).

2. Write the questions on individual index cards, offering four choices for each answer. For example: "Who has been married seven times: (1) Elizabeth Taylor, (2) Mickey Rooney, (3) Gloria Vanderbilt, or (4) Shannon Doherty?"

3. At game time, distribute paper and pencils.

4. Read a trivia question aloud and have Player 1 answer.

5. After Player 1 answers, ask if anyone in the group wants to challenge the answer. If so, let that player offer a different answer. If Player 1 is correct, he or she gets a point, and the player who challenged and was wrong loses a point. If Player 1 is wrong, he or she loses a point, and the challenger gets two points.

6. Continue choosing new players until all the questions are gone.

7. Award a prize to the player with the most points.

Variation

Have a spelling bee contest using stars' names.

Movie Title Charades

This version of Charades is bound to make your party a blockbuster.

Materials Needed

- 40 index cards
- 2 pencils
- Stopwatch or timer

Playing Time: 30–45 minutes

How to Play

1. Divide the players into two teams.

2. Give each team twenty index cards and a pencil and send them to separate rooms. Tell them to think of twenty movie titles for the other team to act out, such as *Gone with the Wind, Babe, Apollo 13, Pulp Fiction, Evita, Jurassic Park, Schindler's List, Mission: Impossible,* and so on. Have them write one title per index card.

3. When both teams are finished, gather them in one room, and have them sit on opposite sides.

4. Have a player from Team 1 draw a card from Team 2's pile.

5. Give the player two minutes to act out the movie title. If Team 1 guesses the title within the two-minute time period, they get a point.

6. When Team 1 is finished, have a player from Team 2 draw a card from Team 1's pile and act out a movie title.

7. Continue alternating teams and players until all the titles are acted out.

8. Award a prize to the team with the most points.

Variation

Instead of acting out movie titles, have players act out specific scenes from selected movies, or, for even more of a challenge, specific characters.

Murder Mystery

Host a Murder Mystery in your party mansion, and let the amateur detectives figure out whodunit.

Materials Needed

- Simple mystery based on ideas from two-minute mystery books or mystery games
- Clues and red herrings to go with the mystery
- Paper
- Pencils, 1 for each player

Playing Time: 30–45 minutes

How to Play

1. Concoct a simple mystery using ideas found in puzzle books or mystery games. For example: There is a dead body in the library, he has bled to death, but there are no murder weapons, only a pool of water beneath the body. How did he die?

2. Set up a crime scene to go with your mystery. For example: Make a body outline with masking tape, and give some clues (a puddle of water) and red herrings (a half-eaten chocolate, a note to a lover, a check made out to a blackmailer, and so on). Close off the crime scene with yellow crepe paper.

3. When players arrive, assign them detective identities, such as Miss Marple, Hercule Poirot, Nancy Drew, Joe Hardy, Cordelia Grey, Sherlock Holmes, Kinsey Milhone, Sam Spade, and so on.

4. Give the players paper and pencils, and let them study the scene.

5. Tell everyone to write down the murderer, weapon, method, and motive.

6. Then have the detectives read their answers aloud (many will be humorous), and see who came closest to solving the mystery.

Variation

Stage a live-action sequence during which someone suddenly drops dead. Then have the players solve the murder.

Mystery Guests

This game is filled with surprises. Can you guess that familiar voice?

Materials Needed

- Curtain
- Paper
- Pencils, 1 for each player

Playing Time: 30–45 minutes

How to Play

1. While making your guest list for the party, select five or six people to be special guests: someone who moved away, someone who is visiting, someone who just got out of the hospital, and so on.

2. Ask the special guests to arrive at the party half an hour early to prepare for their parts. Have them write a short script, offering clues to their identity, a short anecdote or funny story to share, and anything else that might intrigue your quests. Keep the special guests out of sight as the other guests arrive.

3. At game time, draw a curtain across a doorway, so the special guests can stand behind it without being seen by the other players.

4. Distribute paper and pencils.

5. Have the first special guest stand behind the curtain and read his or her script using a disguised voice.

6. Tell the rest of the players to write down who they think the person is.

7. When the special guest is finished talking, let the players shout out their guesses. Then reveal the special guest to see who was right.

Variation

If you have connections to a famous person, include them in the special guest group for an added surprise.

Name That Tune

Do your guests think they know a wide variety of music? Test their skills with a classic game of Name That Tune!

Materials Needed

• Radio
• Paper and pencil to keep score

Playing Time: 30–45 minutes

How to Play

1. Gather the players in a circle around the radio.

2. Tell the players to listen as you slowly turn the dial until you find a station playing music.

3. As soon as the players hear music, have them race to guess the name of the song or the artist.

4. Award a point for each correct answer, keep track of points, and continue moving the dial to the next musical station.

5. If there is an argument about the title or artist of a song, take a vote, or discard the song and move on.

6. Award bonus points if a player knows the song is a remake by a different artist.

7. Award bonus points for any other related information: the year the song was popular, what movie it was in, who wrote it, and so on.

Variation

Instead of using a radio, prerecord sections of a variety of songs on a cassette tape and keep a list of the correct answers. Play them back on a cassette player, pausing a few seconds between songs to allow the players to guess. Award points to the player with the most points.

News Nuts

Some of the things you read in the newspaper are hard to believe. Can you tell the true stories from the fabrications?

Materials Needed

- Book of strange-but-true news stories, available at the library or bookstore
- 40 index cards
- Paper
- Pencils, 1 for each player

Playing Time: 30–45 minutes

How to Play

1. Select twenty of your favorite strange-but-true stories, and write them on index cards—one true story per card.

2. Next, make up twenty stories that are just as strange but aren't true, and write them on index cards—one fabricated story per card.

3. Shuffle the cards and stack them in a pile. Keep track of which stories are true and which are false on a separate answer sheet.

4. Have a player draw a card and read the story to the rest of the group.

5. Tell the players to write down whether they think the story is true or false. Reveal the answer, and give a point for each correct answer.

6. Have the next player draw the next card, read it, and have the rest of the players guess whether the story is true or false.

7. Continue until all the cards have been read and the answers guessed.

8. Award a prize to the player with the most points.

Variation

Read one true story and one false story, then have the group guess which one is true and which one is false.

Noise Maker

Can your friend moo like a cow? Is that your sister or your beeper? Discover the hidden vocal talents of your guests.

Materials Needed

- 20 or 30 index cards
- Paper
- Pencils, 1 for each player

Playing Time: 30–45 minutes

How to Play

1. On individual index cards, write down twenty to thirty items that make distinct noises. For example: car engine, hair dryer, faucet, telephone, beeper, violin, creaky stairs, percolator, fire alarm, computer keyboard, airplane, radio static, thunder, and so on.

2. Stack the index cards facedown. Distribute paper and pencils.

3. Have Player 1 draw the top card, read it without showing it to the other players, and try to duplicate the sound the item makes.

4. Tell the other players to write down what they think the sound is supposed to be.

5. When everyone has guessed, have Player 1 read the item from the card. Give a point for each correct answer.

6. Repeat until all the cards are gone.

7. Award a prize to the player with the most points.

Variation

Have Player 1 make the sound that's written on the card. Then have Player 2 copy that sound, adding the sound that's written on his or her card. Continue until the last player has recalled all the sounds in order, and added his or her own.

Not Me!

If you can't trust your friends to tell you the truth, whom can you trust? Not me!

Materials Needed

• Index cards
• Pencils, 1 for each player

Playing Time: 30–45 minutes

How to Play

1. Distribute three index cards and a pencil to each player, and ask them to write down three little-known facts about themselves—one fact per card. For example, one player might write "I don't like chocolate," "I have an extra toe," "I once met Billy Ray Cyrus." Have them disguise their handwriting.

2. Collect the cards, shuffle them, and place them in a pile.

3. Have Player 1 take the top card and read the fact. (If the fact pertains to Player 1, he or she must reshuffle the card and choose another.)

4. Tell Player 1 to point to the player who wrote the little-known fact. If Player 1 is correct, he or she gets to keep the card and play again. If Player 1 is incorrect, the card is returned to the bottom of the stack. Then Player 2 takes the top card and tries to guess the player who wrote the fact.

5. Continue until all the cards are gone.

6. Award a prize to the player who has the most cards.

Variation

Have a player read the card, and let the other players write down who they think it is. Then have the player who wrote the fact admit the truth. Award points to those who guess correctly.

Now You See It

Now you see it, now you don't—so look quickly before it all disappears.

Materials Needed

- Large photograph, poster, or other detailed picture
- Paper
- Pencils, 1 for each player

Playing Time: 30 minutes

How to Play

1. Select an interesting photograph, poster, or work of art, such as an old group photograph, a poster of a movie star, or a reproduction of a Van Gogh; make sure the picture is large enough for everyone in the group to see clearly.

2. Distribute paper and pencils, and let the players study the picture for thirty seconds.

3. Turn the picture around so it's no longer visible, and ask the players a series of questions about the picture, such as "Who is standing on the left?" "What color are Tom Cruise's eyes?" or "Which ear is missing?" Have the players write down their answers.

4. After you have finished asking the questions and the players have written their answers, turn the picture around and have them check their answers.

5. Award a prize to the player with the most correct answers.

Variation

Cut out a small picture of Waldo and hide him somewhere in the picture. Have the players race to find him.

Obscure Holidays

Don't you wish every day was a holiday? This game makes your wish come true.

Materials Needed

- *Chase Book of Annual Events* or other complete holiday directory
- Index cards
- Paper
- Pencils, 1 for each guest

Playing Time: 30–45 minutes

How to Play

1. Using a holiday directory, collect a list of three obscure holidays per month, such as Millard Fillmore's Birthday, National Hot Dog Day, and Silent Day. Write one holiday per index card. Keep track of their dates on a separate sheet of paper.

2. Distribute paper and pencils.

3. Shuffle the index cards and place them in a pile.

4. Have a player take the top card and read the obscure holiday.

5. Tell all the players to write down in what month the holiday occurs.

6. After all the players have guessed, read the correct answer. Give a point for each correct answer.

7. Continue drawing cards and guessing months until all the cards are gone.

8. Award a prize to the player with the most points.

Variation

Have the players call out the answers instead of writing them down. Have them guess specific dates instead of just the months. Have them explain what the holiday celebrates, if the answer is not obvious from the name.

One-Word Charades

Playing a game of Charades is easy when there are lots of words to act out. But what if there is only one word?

Materials Needed

- 40 index cards
- 2 pencils
- Stopwatch or timer

Playing Time: 45–60 minutes

How to Play

1. Divide the players into two teams and send them to separate rooms.

2. Give each team twenty index cards, and have them write single words on the cards, such as water, between, president, Charades, bacteria, turn, and so on. Any single word is acceptable, except foreign words.

3. Have the teams return to the game room with their cards. Place the cards in separate piles for each team.

4. Have Player 1 from Team 1 draw a card from Team 2's pile.

5. Give Player 1 two minutes to act out the word for his or her team. If Player 1's team guesses the correct word, they get a point.

6. Alternate teams and players until the cards are gone.

7. Award a prize to the team with the most points.

Variation

Restrict the words to one category, such as people, foods, verbs, states, and so on.

Opening Lines

"It was the best of times, it was the worst of times. . . ." depending on whether you knew the correct answer to Opening Lines!

Materials Needed

- A book of famous opening lines, or a collection of popular books, available at the library
- Paper
- Pencils, 1 for each player

Playing Time: 30–45 minutes

How to Play

1. Write down the opening lines from twenty books, such as "In the beginning . . ."*(The Bible)* or "Call me Ishmael" *(Moby Dick)*.

2. Distribute paper and pencils.

3. Read the first opening line aloud, and have the players write down the name of the book.

4. When everyone has guessed, go on to the next opening line and have them write down the next answer.

5. When every opening line has been read and guessed, read the answers. Give a point for each correct answer.

6. Award books as prizes to the players with the most points.

Variation

Select opening lines from books in only one genre, such as mystery, science fiction, or romance. Or limit the books to either current literature or classics.

Panic Word!

Don't panic! All you have to do is think quickly to keep up in this fast-moving word game!

Materials Needed

- 100 index cards
- Pen
- Stopwatch or timer

Playing Time: 45–60 minutes

How to Play

1. Write down 100 single words on index cards. Choose any words you like. For example: blink, stairs, death, lint, computer, listen, corner, and so on.

2. Stack the cards in a pile and place them in the center of the play area.

3. Divide the group into two teams. Seat the players alternately in a circle.

4. Set the timer for one minute and start the game.

5. Have Player 1 from Team 1 draw a card from the pile and give clues to the word to teammates before the timer ends the play. If the word is "blink," the clue may be "What to do if dust gets in your eyes?"

6. Tell players from Team 1 to guess the word. When they do, the player from Team 2 sitting next to Player 1 from Team 1 draws a card and tries to get his or her team to guess the word.

7. Continue playing rapidly around the circle until the timer runs out. If a player is still giving clues when the timer runs out, the other team is awarded a point.

8. Play until all the words are used. Make more words if you want to continue to play.

Variation

Choose words from specific categories, such as people, places, and so on.

Pass or Play

Play this version of the classic television game show *Password,* and try to beat your friends to the right word.

Materials Needed

- Index cards
- Pens or pencils, 1 for every two players

Playing Time: 30–45 minutes

How to Play

1. Divide the players into groups of four, and seat them together at individual tables. Have the players choose partners. Every couple is a team.

2. Place index cards and pens on each table.

3. Have Player 1 from Team 1 write a word on an index card (no foreign words or proper nouns).

4. Tell Player 1 to show the word to Player 1 from Team 2. Player 1 from Team 2 gets to pass or play, which means he or she can pass the turn back to Player 1 from Team 1, or begin the game. If Player 1 from Team 2 decides to play, he or she says a one-word clue to help his or her teammate guess the word written on the index card.

5. If Player 2 from Team 2 guesses the word, Team 2 gets a point. If Player 2 misses the word, Player 1 from Team 1 has a chance to give a one-word clue to his or her partner.

6. Continue playing until one of the teams guesses the word. Award that team a point.

7. Then have Player 2 from Team 1 make up a word, and so on, alternating teams and players.

8. Award a prize to the first pair of players to score ten points.

Variation

Have an emcee make up the words and distribute them to the pairs. Or have a tournament, pitting the winning couples from each table against each other.

Pass the Pretzel

Can the players pass the pretzels without poking their partners? Perhaps!

Materials Needed

• Cotton swabs
• Pretzels (curly not stick)

Playing Time: 20 minutes

How to Play

1. Divide the players into two teams and line them up.

2. Give each player a cotton swab and tell them to put one end of the swab in their mouths. Then ask them to put their hands behind their backs.

3. Give the first player in each line a pretzel by inserting it onto the swab.

4. On the count of three, have the first two players pass the pretzels to the next players in line, using only the cotton swab. If the pretzel falls, the player who dropped it must give it back to the player before him or her, and repeat the play.

5. Award a prize to the team that first passes the pretzel all the way down the line.

Variation

Use Cheerios and toothpicks to make the game more challenging. (Just don't poke an eye out!) Or pass oranges from neck to neck, hats from head to head, or a sheet of paper from chin to chin—all without using hands! (See Scoop-a-Cup, page 128, and Whoops! There It Goes!, page 177, for other variations on this game.)

Penny Bets

Play this game of chance, and let the lucky winners take home a handful of change.

Materials Needed

• Index cards
• Pens in a variety of colors
• Lots of pennies

Playing Time: 1–2 hours

How to Play

1. Select a televised sporting event or an awards program, or rent a favorite video.

2. Place index cards on a table in the screening room, and distribute a different-color pen to each player.

3. Before the show begins, have the players place bets on anything and everything about the upcoming event. For a sporting event, bet on which commercials will be shown, what players will be injured, and who will spit first. For an awards program, bet on the outfits, the speeches, and who's with whom. For a favorite video, bet on specific details (this works best if every player has seen the video).

4. Write the betting categories on index cards and place them in a row on the table. Have each player write a guess on an index card for each betting category and place it in the appropriate pile. (The players should put their name under their guess.)

5. Have players place pennies on the bets. The player who gets the correct answer wins the pile of pennies on that pile of cards.

6. Continue until the show is over or until all the bets have been won.

Variation

Bet with candy instead of pennies—or raise the ante to nickels and dimes.

People Roast

Roast a favorite friend over a roaring hot litany of words, but keep it all in fun! You don't want to burn anyone—just heat 'em up a bit.

Materials Needed

- Index cards
- Pens, 1 for each guest
- Large table with podium for speaker

Playing Time: 45–60 minutes

How to Play

1. Choose a special guest to honor, and ask him or her to come a half hour after everyone else.

2. To make the special guest stand out, ask him or her to wear something casual, such as a Hawaiian shirt and shorts, while asking all the other guests to dress formally in tuxedos and gowns—or vice versa.

3. Set up a table with a podium.

4. When the guests arrive, give them index cards and pens, and ask them to write some funny lines about the special guest. You may want to let the guests see a copy of *The World's Funniest Roast Jokes* from Meadowbrook Press for ideas. Encourage them to tell embarrassing anecdotes and silly stories about the special guest, but make them humorous, not mean-spirited.

5. When the special guest arrives, seat all the guests at the table, with the special guest in the hot seat next to the podium.

6. Begin by having one of the guests make a speech.

7. Continue until all the guests have roasted the special guest.

8. Give the special guest a chance to rebut each speaker.

Variation

Ask the guests to come prepared with a speech, or take turns sitting in the hot seat.

Personal Jeopardy

Show off your knowledge with this home version of the TV game show *Jeopardy*.

Materials Needed
• Index cards
• Paper
• Pen or pencil

Playing Time: 45–60 minutes

How to Play

1. Select a number of categories that are relevant to your group of players, such as home, work, kids, entertainment, cars, vacations, relationships, sports, and so on.

2. Write the categories on index cards.

3. For each category, collect some anecdotes that relate to each topic and that are personal to the group.

4. Use those anecdotes to write five answers related to a topic on individual index cards. For example, if the category is "kids," you might write, "This little boy got a marble stuck in his nose" or "This child sold more scout cookies than the rest of her troop." Keep track of the questions on a separate sheet of paper.

5. Place five category cards on the table or floor in a row where everyone can see them.

6. Under each category, place the index cards with related answers, facedown, to complete your game board.

7. Have the players take turns choosing a category. Begin with the first index card under that category. Read the information on the index card, and ask the players to give their answers in the form of a question. If the player gets the question right, he or she keeps the card and plays again.

8. Continue playing until all the questions are gone. Or set a time limit on the game, as in the TV game.

9. Award a prize to the player with the most cards.

Variation

Instead of personalizing the game, use a variety of questions and answers on general topics.

Personalized Bingo

Why play plain old bingo when you can play the personalized version, in which everyone picks their own squares?

Materials Needed

- 5-by-5-inch poster board squares (2 for each player)
- Fine-point pens, 1 for each player
- Scissors
- Items with which to mark the bingo squares, such as beans, Cheerios, small candies, pennies, and so on

Playing Time: 30–45 minutes

How to Play

1. Make bingo cards by drawing five columns and five rows on the 5-by-5-inch poster board squares. Give one card to each player.

2. Cut the remaining cards into one-inch squares (twenty-five squares per card). Discard one square.

3. Give each player twenty-four small squares and a pen.

4. Choose a theme for the game, such as foods, vacation spots, bad words, movie stars, and so on. Have each player write twenty-four theme-related items on the bingo card, leaving the center "free." Ask the players to keep their cards private until playing time.

5. When finished, tell the players to write the same items on the small squares.

6. Collect all the small squares in a bowl. Mix them up.

7. Take turns drawing a square from the bowl and announcing the item. Everyone with a matching item gets to place a marker on that square.

8. Award a prize to the first player who fills his or her bingo card. Or, if you prefer, only have them fill five squares in a row—up, down, or across—as in regular bingo.

Variation

After players make their personalized bingo cards, have them exchange their cards with other players.

Personal Pursuit

How well do you really know your friends? Find out during an intimate game of Personal Pursuit.

Materials Needed

• Index cards
• Paper
• Pencils, 1 for each player

Playing Time: 45–60 minutes

How to Play

1. Before the party begins, call your guests and ask them four or five questions about their personal histories, such as "What's the most unusual job you've ever had?" "Where did you go on your first date?" and "Where did you have your first sexual experience?" Ask them not to discuss the information with anyone else.

2. Using the information gathered from the phone calls, write multiple-choice questions about all the players, such as "Bruce's most unusual job was (a) bartender, (b) Chippendale dancer, (c) sanitation worker, or (d) publisher." Write one question per index card.

3. Distribute paper and pencils and read the questions to the players. Have them write down their answers.

4. After reading all the questions and giving the players time to write the answers, read the questions again. This time have the guest featured in the question answer it correctly. Give a point for each correct answer.

5. Award a prize to the player with the most points.

Variation

Instead of making up multiple choice questions, make up open-ended questions, such as "Who worked as a Chippendale dancer?" Then let the players guess.

Personals

Your friends desperately need dates, but can they write a personal ad to attract that special someone?

Materials Needed

- Copy of the personals section from any newspaper
- Paper
- Pencils, 1 for each player

Playing Time: 30–45 minutes

How to Play

1. Before the game begins, read the personal ads and circle the ones that are unusual, romantic, exciting, and so on.

2. Distribute paper and pencils.

3. Pass the personal ads around and have the players take turns reading the circled ones aloud to the group.

4. After everyone has heard a sampling of the ads, ask each player to write a personal ad for themselves, capturing their own essence without giving away their identity. The ad must be cryptic, romantic, interesting, alluring, provocative, and compelling.

5. Give the players five or ten minutes, and then collect the personal ads.

6. Mix them up and pass one to each player.

7. Ask the first player to read the ad aloud to the group. Have the rest of the players try to guess who wrote the ad. Give a point for each correct answer.

8. Continue around the circle until all the ads have been read.

9. Award a prize to the player with the most points.

Variation

Make copies of the personal ads for each player. Have them read over the copies and choose one they would pursue. Then have the players guess which ad each player selected.

Physical Description

Those legs! Those eyes! You see your friends all the time, but do you really look at them? Find out with a game of Physical Description!

Materials Needed

• Paper
• Pencils, 1 for each player

Playing Time: 30–45 minutes

How to Play

1. Write down players' names on strips of paper and put them into a bowl. Have each player draw a name.

2. Distribute paper and pencils.

3. Ask each player to write down three positive physical descriptions of the person whose name they drew. Begin with something not too obvious, such as clean nails or long toes. Then write something more obvious, such as glowing cheeks or silky hair. Then make the third item even more obvious, such as freckles or narrow waist.

4. When everyone has written three physical descriptions, have Player 1 read his or her descriptions, beginning with the most obscure physical trait.

5. Tell players to write down to whom they think the physical trait refers.

6. Have Player 1 read the second trait. Players can either leave their original answer or change it to someone new.

7. After the third item is read and players have written a third guess, tell Player 1 to reveal the name of the person described.

8. Give three points to all players who guessed right the first time, two points to those who guessed right the second time, and one point to those who guessed right the third time.

9. Go on to the next player, and so on, until every player has had a chance to read all three descriptions.

10. Award a prize to the player with the most points.

Variation

Instead of physical traits, write down personality traits.

Picture Puzzle Race

All you need are a couple of photographs of your happy group of friends, and you've got yourself a fast-moving game.

Materials Needed

- 2 color copies of a photograph of your group of friends or of an individual from your group, enlarged to 11-by-13 inches or bigger (Ideally, the group picture should contain all the players.)
- 2 sheets of poster board
- Glue or double-sided tape
- 2 large envelopes

Playing Time: 30 minutes

How to Play

1. Before the game begins, mount the enlarged pictures onto poster board with glue or double-sided tape.

2. Cut the pictures into equal numbers of puzzle pieces. Place the puzzle pieces for each picture into a large envelope.

3. At game time, divide the players into two teams.

4. Give each team an envelope containing the puzzle pieces.

5. On the word "Go," tell the players to race to assemble the picture.

6. Award a prize to the team that first completes the puzzle.

Variation

Make puzzles from individual photographs of all your guests, and have them race one another to complete their own puzzles. Then dump all the puzzle pieces into a pile, and have the players try to separate the pieces and reconstruct the original pictures.

Pin the Fig Leaf on the Hunk or Babe

Remember when you played Pin the Tail on the Donkey? We've come a long way, baby! Watch where you stick that pin!

Materials Needed

• Large poster of a favorite star
• Cardboard
• Brown construction paper or real leaves
• Pushpins or thumbtacks
• Blindfold

Playing Time: 20–30 minutes

How to Play

1. Find a sexy poster of your favorite star. If you have a mixed group, select two posters, one male and one female, such as Pamela Anderson, Marilyn Monroe, or Cindy Crawford, and Fabio, James Dean, or Brad Pitt.

2. Mount the posters onto cardboard and hang them on the wall. (Use as much cardboard as you need to protect the wall from holes.)

3. Cut out leaf shapes from construction paper, large enough to cover a favorite or designated body part, or use real leaves (fresh ones that won't crumble).

4. Stick pushpins or thumbtacks into the leaves.

5. Blindfold the players one at a time, give them a leaf, spin them, then aim them in the direction of the poster. Ask them to try to cover their favorite or a designated body part with the leaf.

6. After everyone has had a turn, award a prize (the poster?) to the player who got the closest to the target.

Variation

Draw the body part you want covered, cut it out, and use it instead of a leaf. Or have the players use felt-tip pens to draw body parts on the poster, blindfolded. Or hang up an outline of a body, have guests pick body parts from a hat, then blindfold them, and have them draw the body part onto the outline.

Play it by Ear

It doesn't take talent to play this piano—just a good ear. So listen up and name that tune.

Materials Needed

- Toy piano or xylophone
- Books of piano sheet music, available at a library or music store

Playing Time: 30–45 minutes

How to Play

1. Buy or borrow an inexpensive toy piano or xylophone.

2. Check out a library or music store for books containing sheet music for a variety of popular songs.

3. Gather the guests around the playing area.

4. Give Player 1 the toy piano and the book of sheet music, and have him or her select a song without letting the other players see the selection.

5. Tell Player 1 to bang out the selected tune, following the notes on the sheet music, to the best of his or her ability.

6. Have the rest of the players race to identify the song. Give a point to the first player to name that tune.

7. Switch the musicians and the song. Continue playing the game until everyone has had a turn at the piano.

8. Award a prize to the player with the most points.

Variation

Instead of passing around sheet music, have the pianists wing it, and just play by ear. See if anyone can recognize the tune.

Police Lineup

How does a crook look—beady eyes? crooked smirk? baby face? Examine your friends in this Police Lineup, and see if you can point a finger at the right suspect.

Material Needed

• Index cards
• Paper
• Pencils, 1 for each player

Playing Time: 30–45 minutes

How to Play

1. Before the game begins, write down a simple crime for each player, such as "You stole the King of Hearts' tarts!" "You took candy from a baby!" and "You parked in a handicapped zone!" Write one crime per index card.

2. At game time, give each player a card. Have them read their crime, without sharing them, then write their names on the cards.

3. Collect the cards and place them in a bowl.

4. Pick a card and discreetly check the name on the card. Ask that person and two other players to stand in a lineup and face the group. (When you call up the players for a lineup, alternate the order in which you call them—the "criminal" shouldn't always be first, middle, or last.)

5. Read the crime to the rest of the players, and have each of them ask one question of each of the suspects.

6. Tell the suspects to make up responses to the questions. As they do, players must try to guess, by facial expression and body language, which suspect is the guilty one.

7. After players have written down their guesses, have the criminal confess, then award points to those who guessed the right suspect.

8. Continue playing until everyone has had a turn.

Variation

Take instant photos of each guest as they arrive, and give them a prop to hold as a clue. Then read off the crimes and have the players try to guess from the mug shots who is guilty.

Pumpkin Carving

Pumpkin carving has become quite an art. So arm your guests with pumpkins and carving tools, and let 'em at it!

Materials Needed

• Pumpkins
• Carving tools
• Felt-tip pens or markers, 1 for each team
• Newspaper

Playing Time: 30 minutes

How to Play

1. Divide the group into small teams of two to three players. Give each team a pumpkin, some carving tools, newspaper to cover the table, and a felt-tip pen or marker.

2. Tell the teams they have only thirty minutes to design and carve a creative pumpkin. Then start the time and let them go to it.

3. When time is up, have the teams name their pumpkin creations and put them on display.

4. Award prizes for a number of categories, such as most creative, most bizarre, most obscene, most scary, and so on.

Variation

If you don't have pumpkins, use watermelons, cantaloupes, or other large melons. Or give each player a potato to carve.

Quick Change

How good is your memory? Can you remember details? What if the details change? Find out the answers to these questions with Quick Change.

Material Needed

• Accessories, such as gloves, jewelry, hats, scarves, and so on
• Index cards

Playing Time: 30–45 minutes

How to Play

1. Before the party begins, prepare game instructions on index cards. On each card, write down a request that a player must fulfill when the lights go out. For example: "Remove one article of clothing," "Move one piece of jewelry to another place on your body," "Turn something inside out," "Remove the scarf off your hat and tie it around your neck," and so on.

2. Gather the players in the party room and distribute accessories. If possible, make sure that everyone has a scarf, a hat, two or three pieces of jewelry, and so on.

3. Take one of the instruction cards and mix it in with enough blank index cards to match the number of players.

4. Distribute the cards so that one player gets the card with instructions while the rest of the players get blank cards.

5. When the lights go out, have the player with the instructions quickly do what the card says, before the lights come on again.

6. When the lights come back on, tell all the players to look each other over and try to guess who made a change, and what the change was.

Variation

Give different instructions to each player, and have everyone do something when the lights are out. Then have the players guess what each person did. (See Switch Places, page 146, for another version of this game.)

Quick Draw

Although this game is a lot like Pictionary, there's a catch. Can you draw with your eyes closed?

Materials Needed

• 2 pads of paper
• 2 pencils
• Index cards
• Blindfold
• Stopwatch or timer

Playing Time: 45–60 minutes

How to Play

1. On index cards, write words or phrases, such as bellybutton or rock and roll, for the players to draw. Place the cards in a stack in the middle of the play area.

2. Divide the group into two teams and give each team a pad of paper and a pencil.

3. Give a player from Team 1 two minutes to pick a card, read the word or phrase, put on the blindfold, and try to draw the word or phrase on paper for Team 1 to guess. If the team guesses the correct answer before the time is up, they get a point.

4. Alternate teams and players until all the words are gone.

5. Award a prize to the team with the most points.

Variation

Choose words and phrases within a specific category, such as song or movie titles.

Quoth the Raven

You know you've heard that phrase before, but who said it? That's the question!

Materials Needed

- Book of famous quotations
- Index cards
- Paper
- Pencils, 1 for each player

Playing Time: 30–45 minutes

How to Play

1. Write down twenty or thirty of your favorite quotes on index cards—one quote per card.

2. At game time, distribute paper and pencils, and have the players sit in a circle.

3. Read the first quote and have the players write down the author or speaker of the quote.

4. After all the quotes have been read, read them again and have the group identify them. Give a point for each correct answer.

5. Award a prize to the player with the most points.

Variation

In addition to identifying the quote, have the players identify when or where it was said, if applicable. Or, change the quote slightly and have them write down the quote correctly. For an easier game, read the quote, and have the players choose from three or four answers.

Remote Control

Here's a game for couch potatoes that should give the thumb a real workout.

Materials Needed

• TV and remote control
• VCR and blank videotape

Playing Time: 30–45 minutes

How to Play

1. Prepare for the game by taping bits of TV shows from different channels. Repeat every half hour or so, until you have a collection of forty to fifty program bits, such as a sitcom, news show, tabloid show, talk show, cartoon, kids' show, music show, political show, educational show, nature show, old black-and-white show, and so on.

2. At game time, assemble the players around the television screen.

3. Turn on the TV and VCR, insert the video, and begin showing the tape. Be ready to pause the tape after every program bit.

4. As you play the tape, have the guests race to guess the name of the show aloud. The first player to guess the correct name gets a point.

5. Continue until all the shows have been identified.

6. Award a prize to the player with the most points.

Variation

If you have many channels, you don't need the VCR. Just use the remote control, and keep changing the dial, guessing the shows as they appear. Keep a TV guide handy to verify answers without having to wait for commercial breaks.

Resolutions

This game is perfect for New Year's Eve. Making the resolutions is easy. It's guessing who they belong to that's hard.

Materials Needed

• Index cards
• Pencils, 1 for each player

Playing Time: 30 minutes

How to Play

1. Give each player a pencil and three index cards.

2. Have players write down a resolution or promise on each card.

3. When everyone is finished, collect the cards and shuffle them.

4. Place the cards in a pile facedown.

5. Have one player select a card, read the resolution, and try to guess who wrote it.

6. If the player guesses correctly, he or she gets to keep the card. If the guess is incorrect, the next player gets a chance to guess who wrote the resolution, and so on, until the resolution is guessed.

7. Then have the next player pick a card and try to guess who wrote the resolution.

8. Continue until all the cards are guessed.

9. Award a prize to the player with the most cards.

Variation

Instead of writing personal resolutions, write resolutions appropriate for other players, then guess which ones are supposed to belong to which players.

Road Rally

Your guests don't need fancy sports cars to enjoy a Road Rally. Just hop in the jalopy, the truck, or the ATV, and follow the instructions!

Materials Needed

- Map of local area
- Paper plates
- Felt-tip pen or marker
- Paper
- Pencils, 1 for each team

Playing Time: 1–2 hours

How to Play

1. Before game time, choose a final destination for your party: restaurant, bar, a player's house, or someplace else that's appropriate.

2. Using a map of the local area, trace the route you plan to follow.

3. Drive the route, writing down instructions as you go, such as (1) Turn left out of driveway, (2) Veer right at fork, (3) Take first left.

4. Include a list of questions to be answered along the route, such as "What street intersects Main?" or "What's the name of the school you pass along the way?"

5. Using the felt-tip pen or marker, write further instructions on paper plates, such as "Ignore last instruction!" or "Turn right instead of left on the next intersection!" These instructions should lead the players to the correct destination. Attach the plates to trees or posts in visible spots.

6. At game time, have the guests draw names to pair up as driver and navigator. Give each pair a set of instructions, paper and a pencil to answer your questions, and point out the final destination. Send them on their way, one minute apart, noting the times of departure.

7. As the players arrive at the final destination, note the time for each team. When all have arrived, check the questions and award points for correct answers.

8. Award a prize (a compass, maybe) to the fastest team and to the team with the most points.

Variation

Play the game on foot instead of in the car.

Rob Your Neighbor

It's easy to rob your neighbor, but getting away with it is the hard part.

Materials Needed
- 10 stickers per player
- Index cards

Playing Time: 1–2 hours

How to Play
1. Purchase a set of ten stickers for each player, making each set unique to each player.

2. As each player arrives, place ten identical stickers on his or her back.

3. At game time, give each player an index card. Tell the players they must collect a sticker from each player in the room without getting caught in the act. Once the player has the sticker, he or she can no longer be "caught."

4. Tell the players to place the stolen stickers on their index card.

5. Continue the game throughout the party time, until one player has stolen a sticker from each player.

Variation
Instead of stealing stickers from one another, have players place their personal stickers on all of the other players. The first player who gets rid of all of his or her stickers wins the game.

Romance Writer

How well do you know your romance literature? Can you tell a throbbing thigh from a heaving heart?

Materials Needed

• Romance novels
• Paper
• Pencils, 1 for each player

Playing Time: 30–45 minutes

How to Play

1. Select some hot and steamy passages from popular romance novels—or write your own.

2. Write out the passages, then cross out significant words. For example, in the passage: "He placed his hot, powerful hand on her soft, tingling shoulder, and pulled her lips to his," you may cross out "hand," "shoulder," and "lips."

3. Rewrite the passages on a sheet of paper, leaving a blank line where the words have been crossed off; photocopy the paper for all the players.

4. Distribute the photocopies and pencils and have the players fill in the missing words. For the passage above, someone may write "He placed his hot, powerful *tongue* on her soft tingling *toe*, and pulled her *hair* to his."

5. Go around the room and have players read their completed passages aloud. (You should get some funny, sexy, and silly passages.)

6. If anyone gets the passage correct, award a prize. Also award prizes for the funniest, sexiest, most outrageous, and so on.

Variation

Select passages from science fiction, mystery, or poetry.

Scavenger Bingo

This game will get your guests circulating—all around the house.

Materials Needed

- Bingo-type cards, with 9 to 12 grid squares
- Pens, 1 for each player

Playing Time: 20–30 minutes

How to Play

1. Write down a list of items easily found around your party room, your home, or your yard. For example: rolling pin, flowered throw pillow, laundry basket, bubble bath, napkins, hose, dog dish, and so on.

2. Write the names of the items in the grid squares of the cards. Mix up the order in which you write the items on each card. Make sure that each card has some items that are different from all the other cards.

3. Distribute the cards and pens.

4. Tell the players that they must search the room, house, or yard for each item on the card to win the game. When a player finds an item, he or she should quietly mark the item's location on the card, trying not to give it away to the other players.

5. Award a prize to the player who fills the card first.

Variation

Before game time, place stickers next to each item listed on the cards, and let the guests retrieve a sticker to place on the item-appropriate grid (instead of having the players write down where they find the items). Or have the players find specific items located on other players, such as a Rolex watch, a pair of Birkenstocks, a gold chain, and so on. As the players enter the party, write down something that's on their person to include on the bingo cards. Then prepare the cards, mixing up the items, and distribute them to your guests.

School Daze

Any elementary-school graduate can still recite the ABCs and multiplication tables. But can you remember your teachers' names?

Materials Needed

• Paper
• Pencils, 1 for each player

Playing Time: 20–30 minutes

How to Play

1. Distribute paper and pencils.

2. Tell the players this is a simple game of memory. All they have to do is write down the names of their teachers from kindergarten through high school.

3. Next, tell them to write down their own phone numbers and addresses from childhood.

4. Next, tell them to write down the name of the pets they had when they were children.

5. Next, tell them to write down three gifts they got for Christmas when they were in elementary school.

6. Next, tell them to write down three costumes they wore for Halloween during elementary school.

7. Finally, tell them to write down the names of three friends they had in elementary school but whom they no longer see.

8. Tally up the answers, trusting that everyone told the truth, and award a prize for the best recall.

Variation

Add more questions about childhood memories, such as names of your principals, when you learned to ride a bike, your worst mischief, the first time you tried a cigarette, your entire family's birthdays, how and when you got your first traffic ticket, and so on.

Scoop-a-Cup

How many ways can you transport various items from point A to point B without spilling?

Materials Needed

- Variety of objects to use for transporting items, such as a cookie sheet, hat, large cardboard box, spatula, baster, gloves, and so on
- Variety of awkward items to transport, such as water, feathers, rice, peas, coins, and so on
- Rope or masking tape

Playing Time: 30–45 minutes

How to Play

1. Pair transportation objects with items to be transported. The pairing should make transporting difficult but not impossible. For example, you may pair a cookie sheet with water, a hat with feathers, a large cardboard box with a tiny grain of rice, a spatula with peas, a baster with water, gloves with a coin, and so on.

2. Divide the players into two teams. Line them up on one side of the room.

3. Mark the goal line with rope or masking tape.

4. Give a player from each team one transporter and an item to transport. On the word "Go," have them race to get the items to the goal line and back. If they drop the item along the way, they must return to the starting point and race again.

5. When the first set of players returns with their items, tell them to tag the next two players, who then pick up the next two transporters and the items to transport and race to the goal line and back.

6. Continue playing until all items have been transported.

7. Award a prize to the team that finishes first.

Variation

Blindfold the players, of course! (See Pass the Pretzel, page105, and Whoops! There It Goes!, page 177, for other variations on this game.)

Scrabble around the World

Play the foreign language version of Scrabble and learn a new vocabulary as you scramble for points.

Materials Needed

- Scrabble game
- Foreign language dictionaries (only languages with an alphabet similar to English)
- Pencil and paper to keep score

Playing Time: 45–60 minutes

How to Play

1. Set up the Scrabble game according to the rules included with the game.

2. Tell players they may not use any English words, only foreign words. Any foreign language with an alphabet similar to English is acceptable, as long as there is a dictionary available for translation, in case of a challenge.

3. Have Player 1 begin the game by placing letters in the center of the board that spell a word in a foreign language. If any other players doubt the word, they can challenge it, then look it up in the foreign dictionary. If the word is not there, Player 1 retracts the letters and loses that turn. If the word is indeed in the dictionary, the player who challenged loses a turn.

4. Continue playing, adding up points according to the rules, until the letters have been used up.

Variation

Play using only one language (other than English), or play using only slang words, pig Latin, nonsense words that sound like real words, and so on.

Scramble

The premise seems easy—just pick out your own stuff from a pile of items. But what if your stuff looks like everybody else's?

Materials Needed

- 3 personal items from each player (brush, comb, wallet, checkbook, key chain, lipstick, gum, and so on)
- Stopwatch or timer

Playing Time: 20–30 minutes

How to Play

1. Ask players to pull out three things from their pockets and/or purses and place them in the center of the play area.

2. Give players thirty seconds to retrieve their own items from the pile.

3. A player who retrieves his or her three items before the time is up wins a prize. If no one gets three items by the end of the time period, everything is returned to the pile, and the game is played again.

4. After a player has won, change the game, assigning different items to each player. For example, have a player try to snatch one player's wallet, another player's lipstick, and another player's key chain.

Variation

Blindfold the players and have them retrieve their items by feel alone.

Secret Pal

Who's your secret party pal? Your party pal will never tell, but you can try to guess!

Materials Needed

• Index cards

Playing Time: 1–2 hours

How to Play

1. Write the names of each guest on separate index cards. Fold and staple them shut, and place them in a bowl or box.

2. As your guests arrive, have each of them pick a card and open it.

3. Tell them that on the card is the name of their secret party pal and they must do five special things for their pal during the evening, without getting caught. For example, they may replace an empty drink, slip a special note under their dinner plate, compliment them on their hair, offer to share an appetizer, or anonymously nominate the party pal for some special award.

4. Tell everyone to figure out the identity of their secret party pal by the end of the party.

5. At the end of the evening, have everyone guess who their secret pals are, and then reveal their identities.

Variation

Tell the guests ahead of time who their secret pals are, so they can prepare surprises, tactics, and/or gifts for their pals.

Secrets

Everyone has a secret, but can you differentiate between secrets and lies?

Materials Needed

• Paper
• Pencils, 1 for each player

Playing Time: 30–45 minutes

How to Play

1. Give each player three sheets of paper and a pencil.

2. Ask them to write down one secret they haven't shared (one they don't mind sharing with the group) and two made-up secrets.

3. When everyone has written three secrets, have Player 1 begin the game by reading, in random order, his or her three secrets.

4. Tell the players to guess which of the three secrets is true and to write down the answer.

5. When everyone has guessed, have Player 1 reveal the true secret.

6. Award points to the players who guessed correctly.

Variation

Have each player write each secret (true and made-up) on an index card, collect all the cards, shuffle them, and place them in a bowl or box. Draw one card at a time, read it aloud to the group, and tell the players to guess who told the secret, and whether it is true.

Self-Portrait

How well do you really see yourself? How about when your eyes are closed?

Materials Needed

- Large sheets of white paper
- Pencils, 1 for each player
- Blindfolds, 1 for each player

Playing Time: 20–30 minutes

How to Play

1. Give each player a large sheet of paper and a pencil.

2. Blindfold each player or have them close their eyes.

3. Tell the player to draw self-portraits without looking in a mirror or at the paper.

4. Collect the portraits as they are completed, without letting anyone else see the finished work.

5. When everyone is finished, show the portraits one at a time and have the players guess who's who.

Variation

Have players draw celebrities, such as Madonna, President Clinton, Beavis or Butthead, and so on. Then hold them up and let the other players guess the subject of the portrait.

Sex Education

Test your S.Q.—your sex quotient—and dazzle (or shock) your friends with the depth of your knowledge.

Materials Needed

• Up-to-date sex manual or book of questions about sex
• Paper
• Pencils, 1 for each player

Playing Time: 45–60 minutes

How to Play

1. Using sex books as a reference, collect fifty questions about a subject you think may stump your guests. For example: "Where is the G-spot?" "What are your chances of getting pregnant while using the withdrawal method?" "What is Depo-Provera?" "When does a woman reach her sexual peak?" "When does a man?" "How many sperm does a man produce in his lifetime?" "How many women have had extramarital affairs?" and so on.

2. Distribute paper and pencils, and read the questions to the group. Have them write down their answers.

3. When all the questions have been read, and all the players have written their answers, read the questions a second time, and have the players give their answers. You should get some funny answers along with the correct answers.

4. Award a sex toy to the player with the most correct answers.

Variation

Have a sex-education bee: Have all players stand up and ask each player a question. Every players who misses an answer must sit down. Continue playing until only one player remains standing.

Shout

If you can out-shout your opponents, you just might win this noisy game.

Materials Needed

- Paper
- Pencil or pen
- 20 small bean bags, balls, or other items you can toss

Playing Time: 30–45 minutes

How to Play

1. Write down a number of categories, such as vegetables, flowers, states, desserts, cars, clothing, furniture, and so on. List ten items that fit each category. For example, for vegetables you may list beans, carrots, peas, zucchini, onions, potatoes, corn, celery, pumpkins, and cucumbers.

2. Divide the group into two teams and line up the teams on either side of the room.

3. Read the first category aloud and tell team members to shout out items in that category.

4. Listen to the teams as they shout out the words, and toss bean bags or balls to the players who shout an answer that matches your list. The first team to receive ten bean bags wins the round.

5. Continue playing by announcing another category.

Variation

Instead of shouting, have the team members write the items on a large sheet of paper. The first team to list all ten items on your list wins the round.

Sign Language

Not everybody knows sign language, but everybody knows body language. So speak up, and see how well you communicate without saying a word!

Materials Needed

- Index cards
- Paper and pencil to keep score
- Stopwatch or timer

Playing Time: 30–45 minutes

How to Play

1. Write down a number of situations or events on index cards for players to act out. For example, you may include landing on the moon, the president getting hit by a golf ball, a kid opening a birthday present, a teenager who is breaking up with a boyfriend or girlfriend, a skiing accident, a scene from a movie, and so on.

2. Shuffle the cards and place them in a bowl or box.

3. Divide the players into two teams.

4. Have Player 1 from Team 1 choose a card and silently read the situation or event.

5. Give Player 1 two minutes to act out the situation or event for his or her teammates to guess.

6. If the teammates guess correctly, award a point to the team.

7. Alternate between teams and players until all the cards are gone.

8. Award a prize to the team with the most points.

Variation

Make the situations or events more complicated. For example: "You've decided to rearrange all the furniture without consulting your spouse. The spouse comes home late in the evening, doesn't turn on the light to avoid waking you up, and stumbles over everything."

Silver Palate

If you have any taste at all, you'll be a winner in the Silver Palate game.

Materials Needed

- Variety of unusual foods, such as guava, caviar, blue corn chips, flan, curried rice, sweetbreads, haggis, buttermilk, and so on (available at supermarkets, gourmet grocery stores, or specialty food shops)
- Plates or bowls
- Aluminum foil
- Paper
- Pencils, 1 for each player

Playing Time: 30–45 minutes

How to Play

1. Place each food item on a plate or in a bowl and cover the container with aluminum foil so the food is not visible.

2. Ask the players to close their eyes (no peeking!).

3. Pass the first food item from player to player and have everyone taste it.

4. Once every player has tasted the food, have them write down what they think it is.

5. When all the foods have been tasted, and all the players have written down their guesses, reveal the food items and have the players read their answers. Give a point for each correct answer.

6. Award a prize to the player with the most points.

Variation

Have an all-candy-bar taste test: Chop a variety of candy bars into tiny bits. Then have the players taste the candy bits and guess what they are.

Six Degrees of Kevin Bacon

Play the game that's sweeping Hollywood. If you're a movie buff, you'll make all the right connections in this game.

Materials Needed

- Paper
- Pencils, 1 for each player
- Pictures of movie stars from magazines, or index cards

Playing Time: 30–45 minutes

How to Play

1. Cut out pictures of movie stars from magazines and spread them out in the center of the play area. Or write celebrities' names on index cards and pile them in the center.

2. Distribute paper and pencils, and seat the players around the pictures or cards.

3. Have Player 1 select a picture of a star or draw an index card.

4. Have Player 2 select a picture or card. Make sure all the players see the pictures or cards.

5. Tell all the players to connect the two celebrities via other stars that have appeared in movies with them. For example, if you select Kevin Bacon and Jamie Lee Curtis, you might pair up Kevin Bacon and Tom Hanks in *Apollo 13,* Hanks and Meg Ryan in *Sleepless in Seattle,* Ryan and Kevin Kline in *French Kiss,* and Kline and Jamie Lee Curtis in *A Fish Called Wanda,* thereby making the connection in four degrees.

6. Give a point to the player who makes the connection first.

7. Have another two players choose pictures or cards and continue playing.

8. After all the pictures or cards are gone, award a prize to the player with the most points.

Variation

To make the game easier, plan out the connections ahead of time on a chart and have the guests fill in the blanks.

Something's Wrong

Your eyes tell you something is wrong with the picture, but will your brain tell you what it is?

Materials Needed

- 20 pictures of familiar people, places, and things
- Scissors, glue, pen
- Paper
- Pencils, 1 for each player

Playing Time: 30–45 minutes

How to Play

1. Before the game begins, find twenty pictures of familiar people, places, or items. For example: a movie star, such as Julia Roberts or Brad Pitt; a travel location, such as New York City or Hawaii; or an everyday item, such as a box of cereal or a car.

2. Change one part of the picture, using scissors, glue, a pen, and so on. For example, you might rearrange a hair style on a movie star, cut the top off a landmark building, or add an extra cartoon character to a product.

3. Photocopy the pictures so the changes won't be obvious.

4. At game time, distribute paper and pencils to all the players.

5. Pass around one picture and ask the players to write down what they think is wrong with it.

6. After all the pictures have been passed around and the changes written down, reveal the actual changes. Give a point for each correct answer.

7. Award a prize to the player with the most points.

Variation

Cut up face photographs of movie stars. Exchange eyes, noses, or mouths, and have the players guess which item belongs to which movie star.

Song Lyrics

Who hasn't had a song play over and over in your head? While some song lyrics are very familiar, can you always name the song those lyrics come from?

Materials Needed

- Variety of music from the radio, cassette tapes, or CDs
- Paper
- Pencils, 1 for each player

Playing Time: 30–45 minutes

How to Play

1. Before the game begins, listen to a variety of songs and write down some of the lyrics from the middle of each song. Make sure you also write down the song titles.

2. At game time, distribute paper and pencils.

3. Read the lyrics to the first song and ask the players to write down the name of the song.

4. When all the lyrics have been read, give the correct names of the song titles. Give points for each correct answer.

5. Award a prize to the player with the most points.

Variation

Write down the lyrics from the beginning of a song. Read one word at a time, allowing players to guess the titles after each word given. The player to guess the title first gets a point.

Sound It Out

Hop Pepper Date Two Ewe. If you listen carefully, that phrase will sound familiar. But what exactly does it mean?

Materials Needed

- Index cards
- Paper
- Pencils, 1 for each players

Playing Time: 30–45 minutes

How to Play

1. Give each player five index cards, paper, and a pencil.

2. On the paper, ask each player to write down five familiar phrases, such as "happy birthday to you," "painted into a corner," "tomorrow is another day," and so on.

3. On the index cards, ask players to translate the familiar phrases into new, individual words that sound the same. For example, you might translate "Happy Birthday to You" into "Hop Pepper Date Two Ewe."

4. When players have translated the five phrases, collect the cards, shuffle them, and place them facedown in a stack.

5. Have a player pick a card and read it aloud to the group.

6. Tell the players to identify the original phrase. Give a point to the player who first correctly calls out the original phrase. (The player who wrote the card must, of course, keep quite while the others guess.)

7. Continue drawing cards and calling out the answers.

8. Award a prize to the player with the most points.

Variation

Instead of reading a card aloud, have the players read it silently and sound it out in their minds.

Speedy Simon

When you play the kids' version of Simon Says in hyperspeed, it becomes a fast-paced adult game of Speedy Simon!

Materials Needed

• Paper
• Pen

Playing Time: 30 minutes

How to Play

1. Before game time, make a list of physical actions.

2. Choose a player to be Simon.

3. Ask the rest of the players to stand in a line facing Simon.

4. Place the list of actions on a chair in front of Simon for easy reference, in case Simon needs some help.

5. Tell Simon to order the players to perform a series of tasks, increasing the speed of the requests and movements over time.

6. If Simon says "Simon says" before a request, the players are to copy the movement. If Simon doesn't say "Simon says," they must not copy the movement. If they do, they are out of the game.

7. Continue until only one player remains to follow Simon's instructions.

8. Award a prize to the remaining player, and make him or her the next Simon.

Variation

Tell Simon to try to fool the other players by telling them to do one task, such as "Put your hands on your ears," while demonstrating another task, such as covering his or her nose. Watch how many players follow the gestures instead of the words. If they do, they are out of the game.

Sports Almanac

This game is for sports lovers only. All you need is a good collection of sports trivia.

Materials Needed

• Sports almanac or other trivia book
• Index cards
• Paper
• Pencils, 1 for each player

Playing Time: 30-45 minutes

How to Play

1. Gather sports questions from a sports almanac and write them on index cards—one question per card. For example: "How many times have the Giants won the World Series?" "Which athlete plays both baseball and football?" "What's the name of the San Jose Shark's coach?" and so on.

2. Write the answers on a separate sheet of paper and set it aside.

3. Distribute paper and pencils.

4. Read the trivia questions to the players and ask them to write down their answers.

5. When all the questions have been read, announce the answers. Give a point for each correct answer.

6. Award a prize to the player with the most points.

Variation

Choose any subject for a trivia game, such as music, food, travel, films, cars, art, and so on.

Superstitions

What happens if you break a mirror when a black cat crosses your path while you're walking under a ladder on Friday the 13? Play this game, and you will find out.

Materials Needed

• Book of superstitions
• Paper
• Pencils, 1 for each player

Playing Time: 30 minutes

How to Play

1. Write down a series of questions based on superstitions, wives' tales, urban legends, folklore, and so on. For example: "What happens if you eat strawberries while you're pregnant?" (The baby will have a birthmark.) "What happens if you break a mirror?" (You will have seven years of bad luck.) "What should you do if you spill salt?" (Throw it over your shoulder.) "What happens if you go swimming after you eat?" (You will have cramps.)

2. Distribute paper and pencils.

3. Read the questions one at a time. Ask the players to write down their answers.

4. Read the questions a second time, and ask the players to share their answers. (You should have some funny ones.) Give a point for each correct answer.

5. Award a prize to the player with the most points.

Variation

Ask the players to explain the superstition's origins. Or, ask players to write one real superstition and one fake superstition. Collect the superstitions, read them aloud, and have players determine which superstitions are real, and which ones are fake.

Surprise!

Here's a game to play on your guests that will keep the party full of surprises!

Materials Needed

- Items necessary for each surprise (See examples in Step 1.)
- Paper
- Pencils, 1 for each player

Playing Time: 1–2 hours

How to Play

1. Create a number of surprises for your guests to encounter throughout the evening. For example: special guest, funny phone call, unexpected pizza delivery, sudden announcement, cake with prizes inside, shocking outfit, lottery or raffle draw, and so on.

2. Prepare the surprises so that one occurs every fifteen to twenty minutes.

3. When all the surprises have been revealed, distribute paper and pencils, and ask the players to write down all the surprises that took place during the evening.

4. Award a surprising prize to the player who remembers all the surprises.

Variation

Ask the guests to bring one surprise to the party and to spring it on the guests during the evening. At the end of the evening, have everyone count the surprises and try to match each surprise with each guest.

Switch Places

While most people can often vividly remember an event from the distant past, short-term visual memory can be fleeting. Just try Switch Places.

Materials Needed

• Various props, such as hats, magazines, drinks, purses, coats, shoes, and so on

Playing Time: 30–45 minutes

How to Play

1. Ask the players to find a spot to sit down.

2. Ask Player 1 to leave the room for a few moments.

3. While Player 1 is gone, ask two players to switch places.

4. Ask Player 1 to return and guess what's different about the group. Give hints if necessary.

5. When Player 1 guesses correctly, have Player 2 leave the room. This time have several people change places.

6. As the game progresses, increase the difficulty by adding props, taking props away, switching more people, and so on.

Variation

Turn out the lights for thirty seconds. While the lights are out, ask all the players to move to a different position. Quiz the group on the changes. (See Quick Change, page 118, for another version of this game.)

Table Manners

We all like to think we don't eat like pigs, but are our manners that impeccable? Get those elbows off the table!

Materials Needed

- Formal table setting for each guest
- Paper
- Pencils, 1 for each guest

Playing Time: 1–2 hours

How to Play

1. When planning a dinner party, ask your guests to come in formal dress.

2. Set a formal place setting at the table for each guest. For tips on formal settings, check out a library book by Martha Stewart or some other dining expert.

3. When all the guests have arrived, tell them they must use their best manners throughout the dinner, beginning with an escort to the table. If any player catches another player breaking the rules of etiquette, the offending player loses a point. Give each player paper and a pencil and ask them to keep track of their own lost points.

4. Continue the game throughout dinner and dessert.

5. At the end of the game, count the points lost by each player, and award a prize to the player who lost the least.

Variation

Designate one player as the Etiquette Police, and have him or her sit at the table and quietly deduct points from the players who break the rules. At the end of the dinner, he or she reads the list of infractions for each player and announces a winner.

Tabloid News

They say you can't believe everything you see in print. But how much can you guess from a headline?

Materials Needed

• Tabloid newspapers
• Scissors and glue
• Paper
• Pencils, 1 for each player

Playing Time: 30–45 minutes

How to Play

1. Read a few tabloids and note what each story is *really* about. For example, if the headline reads: "Roseanne loses fifty pounds in five minutes!" you might think it's a story about Roseanne's diet tips, but, in fact, maybe Roseanne had a leg amputated, or maybe she lost her fifty-pound dog.

2. Select the headlines that are open to interpretation, cut them out, and glue them onto sheets of paper.

3. At game time, distribute paper and pencils.

4. Hold up one of the headlines and ask the players to guess what the story is really about and to write down their answers.

5. After all the headlines have been read, hold up the headlines once again, have the players read their answers, and announce the truth about each story. Give a point for each correct answer.

6. Award a prize to the player with the most points.

Variation

Ask the players to write short articles to fit the headlines.

Take My Advice

People love to give advice, but they don't usually like to take it. Take My Advice offers some interesting give-and-take!

Materials Needed

• Paper
• Pencils, 1 for each player

Playing Time: 30–45 minutes

How to Play

1. Give each player a sheet of paper and a pencil, and ask them to sit in a circle.

2. Ask each player to write at the top of their paper a difficult problem that needs solving. The problems can be real or made-up.

3. Have the players pass their papers to the next player in the circle.

4. Then have each players read the problem written on the paper and write a short solution underneath the problem. Solutions can be sincere or humorous.

5. After everyone has written a solution to the problem, ask the players to fold the papers to that the problem is still visible, but the solution is hidden.

6. Once the papers are folded, have the players pass them to the next player in the circle.

7. Have players read the problems and write their solutions underneath. When finished, have them fold over the solutions and pass the papers one more time.

8. After the papers have been passed three times, pass them again, then have the players read the problems and solutions aloud to the group. You should get a few laughs and maybe some good advice.

Variation

For added adult fun, have the group write embarrassing sex problems for other players to solve.

Talk, Talk, Talk

This one looks easy—all you have to do is talk, but watch what you say or you'll have to shut up!

Materials Needed

- 26 index cards
- Pen or pencil
- Tennis ball

Playing Time: 30–45 minutes

How to Play

1. Write a letter of the alphabet on each index card, and shuffle them.

2. Seat the players in a circle around the stack.

3. Ask Player 1 to draw a card and announce the letter on the card. That letter cannot be used in any word spoken during the first round of the game. For example, if the letter *h* is picked, players may not say any word that contains that letter, such as "he," "when," or "though."

4. Give Player 1 the tennis ball, and have him or her to start a conversation or story by saying one word, being careful not to use the chosen letter.

5. As soon as Player 1 says the first word, tell him or her to toss the ball to another player. That player must continue the story with another word, again being careful not to say a word with the chosen letter. For example, since Player 1 can't say "There" or "The," Player 1 might begin the story with "A." Player 2 continues with "dog," then tosses the ball to Player 3, who says "who." Uh-oh! At that moment, Player 3 is out of the game because he or she said a word that contains the letter *h*.

6. Continue playing by choosing new letters for new rounds.

Variation

Instead of using a ball, tell Player 1 to begin the story, and have the player on Player 1's left add a word, and so on. Give the players a time limit, like three seconds, to think of a word. (See Don't Say It!, page 41, for another version of this game.)

Talk the Talk

Are you keeping up with today's modern lingo? This game will test your communication skills.

Materials Needed

• Dictionary of modern terms and slang
• Paper
• Pencils, 1 for each player

Playing Time: 30–45 minutes

How to Play

1. Using a dictionary of modern terms, jot down the words or phrases that have become popular in the past year or so. For example: spin doctor, downsizing, cruise the net, AbFab, web crawler, treadmill, ATV, and so on.

2. At game time, distribute pencils and paper.

3. Read one of the words and have the players write down a definition and a sentence that contains the word.

4. Continue until all the words have been read.

5. Have players go around the room reading their definitions and sample sentences for each word. Give a point for each correct answer.

6. Award a prize to the player with the most points.

Variation

Use words exclusive to a particular group, such as surfer words, police jargon, computer talk, and so on.

Taste of America

What flavor does Louisiana have? Can you identify New Orleans by taste? See if you can guess foods from across the nation.

Materials Needed

- Unusual regional American dishes, such as sweet potato pie, jambalaya, cioppino, hominy grits, haggis, gefilte fish, and so on
- Copies of the recipes, 1 for each player
- Plates and eating utensils
- Paper
- Pencils, 1 for each player

Playing Time: 1–2 hours

How to Play

1. Before the party, ask each guest to bring an unusual dish that reflects a particular American region or culture. Ask them to bring copies of the recipe for all the guests.

2. Have the guests set the food dishes on the counter or table, keeping the recipes hidden. Ask them not to say anything about the foods to the rest of the players.

3. Offer plates and ask guests to sample each dish.

4. As they sample the selection, ask them to write down what they think the dish is and what the ingredients are.

5. When everyone is finished with the meal, have the guests identify their dishes, list the ingredients, and hand out the recipes.

6. Have the players check their papers to see how many dishes they identified correctly and how many ingredients they named. Give a point for each correct answer.

7. Award a prize to the player with the most points.

Variation

Have an international meal instead of a national one. Assign each guest a country or a culture, and ask them to bring a dish representative of their assigned region.

Teen Talk

It's strange that teenagers are asked to learn a foreign language in school since they already speak one—Teen Talk. See if you can interpret.

Materials Needed

- A collection of 20 to 30 teenage slang words or phrases, acquired from your children or local teenagers
- Index cards
- Paper
- Pencils, 1 for each player

Playing Time: 30 minutes

How to Play

1. Interview a number of teenagers, and ask them for slang words and phrases that are in current use. You might hear such words as "phat" (trendy), "Audi" (I'm leaving), "psych" (I was kidding), "way" (yes, it's true), "homey" (friend), "mosh pit" (dancing area), and so on.

2. Write down the words on index cards. Write the meanings on a separate sheet of paper.

3. At game time, distribute paper and pencils.

4. Ask a player to draw a card and read the word to the group.

5. Have all the players write down the definition of the word and a sentence that contains that word.

6. When all the words have been translated, read them again, and ask the players to read their definitions and sample sentences. Give a point for each correct definition.

7. Award a prize to the player with the most points.

Variation

Give each player three or four index cards that contain slang words or phrases, and have them try to carry on a normal conversation using the slang on their cards.

That's the Way it Was

How well do your friends know recent history? Here's a fun way to remember what's been happening—and when.

Materials Needed

- Year-end guides to past events, found in December and January issues of magazines or newspapers, or in books available at the library
- Construction paper
- Glue or tape
- Paper
- Pencils, 1 for each player

Playing Time: 20–30 minutes

How to Play

1. Research the past year and find twelve major events—one from each month—such as a natural disaster, political coup, business failure, sex scandal, Hollywood surprise, popular person's death, and so on.

2. Write each event on a separate sheet of construction paper, and glue or tape relevant pictures to the each sheet, if possible.

3. Write down the dates for each event on a separate sheet of paper, coded so you can correlate the dates to the events.

4. Distribute pencils and paper.

5. Hold up a sheet of paper with an event, and ask the players to write down when the event occurred during the past year. Have them write down the month and the date, in case of a tie.

6. After you've displayed all twelve events and the players have guessed the dates of each, reveal the actual dates. Give a point for each correct answer.

7. Award a prize to the player with the most points.

Variation

Hand out index cards, and have the players write down a significant event in his or her life. For example: wedding, birth of a child, moving to the community, and so on. Collect the cards, shuffle them, and read them one at a time. Have the players guess the date of the event. Or have the players write down the event and the date, and have the rest of the players guess the person to whom the event belongs.

Think Fast

You'll need coordination and mental agility to play this fast-paced game. Can you catch a ball and answer a question simultaneously?

Materials Needed

• Tennis ball or other kind of ball

Playing Time: 30–45 minutes

How to Play

1. Seat the players in a circle on the floor or chairs.

2. Give Player 1 the ball, and ask him or her to choose a category, such as vegetables, clothing, cars, constellations, and so on.

3. Have Player 1 announce the category and toss the ball to Player 2, who must catch the ball and say an item that fits the announced category. If Player 2 cannot think of an item fast enough, or misses the ball, he or she is out. If Player 2 answers correctly, he or she gets to toss the ball to another player.

4. Continue playing until only one player remains.

5. Award a prize to the winner; play again with a new category.

Variation

Play outside with a water balloon to raise the stakes. Or increase the pace by playing with two or three balls at the same time. If you like, have each player choose a new category before tossing the ball, so other players don't have time to plan an answer.

This Is Your Life

The preparations for this game take quite a bit of planning, but the results are memorable.

Materials Needed
- Cassette recorder and blank tape
- Black construction paper and white poster board
- Notebook
- Pen

Playing Time: 1 hour

How to Play

1. Choose the lucky guest of honor for your party.

2. Find out which friends and relatives the guest hasn't seen for a while, such as a grandparent, cousin, old neighbor, friend from college, former coworker, and so on.

3. Invite the selected friends and relatives to come to the party early, before the guest of honor arrives.

4. Cut out silhouettes of their profiles from black paper and mount them on white poster board.

5. Tape-record their voices as they recall a fond or funny memory.

6. Keep the guests hidden until everyone else has arrived.

7. Read a brief and mysterious introduction to the first surprise guest. Display the silhouette, then play the tape-recorded message.

8. Have the guest of honor try to guess who the mystery guest is.

9. Bring out the mystery guest for a surprise reunion.

10. Continue with the next mystery guest.

Variation
If the mystery guests live far away and can't come to the party, call them and record their voices over the telephone.

Thumbs Up, Thumbs Down

Play this Siskel and Ebert game of likes and dislikes to see whether you and your partner agree or disagree.

Materials Needed

• Index cards
• Paper
• Pen

Playing Time: 30–45 minutes

How to Play

1. Make a list of items that can be evaluated by the players. For example: controversial movie stars, such as Madonna or Pee-wee Herman; mixed-review movies, such as *Mars Attacks* or *Reservoir Dogs;* songs or singers, such as the macarena or Barry Manilow; foods, such as succotash or liver; clothing, such as exercise thongs or platform shoes; fads, such as the Chia Pet or rowing machines; styles, such as pierced navels or tattoos, and so on.

2. Write each topic on an index card, shuffle the cards, and stack them in a pile.

3. Pair up the players and have them sit back to back.

4. Draw a card and read the topic. Both players in Pair 1 must instantly make a thumbs up or thumbs down sign, depending on how each player feels about the topic. For example, if the player likes Madonna, he or she gives a thumbs up. If the player dislikes Madonna, he or she gives a thumbs down. If the players' answers match, the pair gets a point.

5. Move on to the next pair, and then the next, and so on. Continue playing until the cards are gone.

Variation

Have all the pairs play at the same time.

Trace the Body

Can you identify your friends from a body outline at a crime scene?

Materials Needed

- Sheets of paper, approximately 6 feet long by 4 feet wide (tape sheets of paper together, if necessary)
- Felt-tip pen
- Paper
- Pencils, 1 for each player

Playing Time: 30 minutes

How to Play

1. As the guests arrive, take them aside and have them lie down on the paper. Outline their bodies with the felt-tip pen.

2. Hang the body outlines on the wall or lay them out on the floor.

3. Distribute paper and pencils.

4. Have the players guess which body outline belongs to which player, and tell them to write down their answers.

5. When everyone has guessed, match the outlines with the players. Give a point for each correct match.

6. Award a prize to the player with the most points.

Variation

Have the players look over the body outlines and guess their owners. Then add one distinguishing mark, article of clothing, or other identifying item to the outline and have the players guess again. Give extra points to the players who guessed correctly the first time.

Travel Log

Lost in the jungle? Couldn't find your way out of a paper bag? You'll need more than a compass to help you out in this game!

Materials Needed

• Map of an unfamiliar area
• Red pens, 1 for each player

Playing Time: 30–45 minutes

How to Play

1. Find a map of an area unfamiliar to your guests, and photocopy it for all the players.

2. On each map, use a red pen to circle a starting point—the same one for all players.

3. Distribute the maps and red pens.

4. Have the players place their pens on the starting point. Then give directions from the starting point leading to a secret destination, one step at a time, without naming any of the streets, towns, and so on. Use such directions as "Take the first left," "Go three-tenths of a mile and make a U-turn," "Cross over the second river and go east," and so on.

5. When, according to your directions, the players should have reached the secret destination, have them hold up their maps and see if they arrived at the correct place.

6. Award prizes to the players who followed the instructions correctly.

7. Distribute a new set of maps and play again.

Variation

Instead of one person calling out directions, have each player take a turn giving instructions, then compare maps at the end to see if everyone ended up in the same place.

Trivia Bee

In Trivia Bee, just like in the old-fashioned spelling bee, you have to stand and deliver or you're out of the game!

Materials Needed

- 100 index cards
- Book of trivia questions

Playing Time: 30–45 minutes

How to Play

1. Write down one hundred or more trivia questions on index cards. You can make the questions general, topical, personal, or limited to one category. Write the answers on the backs of the index cards.

2. Shuffle the cards and stack them in a pile, the questions faceup and the answers facedown.

3. Have the players stand in a circle.

4. Tell Player 1 to draw a card and answer the trivia question. If Player 1 answers correctly, he or she gets to remain standing, and Player 2 draws a card and tries to answer the question. If a player misses the question, he or she is out of the game and must sit down.

5. Continue until only one player remains standing. That player is declared the Trivia Bee Winner and gets a prize.

Variation

If a player misses a question, have him or her do a stunt before sitting down.

Truth or Dare

This classic game is not just for kids anymore. Play only if you dare.

Materials Needed

• Index cards
• Pen or pencil
• Items required to perform silly stunts (See Step 2.)

Playing Time: 30–45 minutes

How to Play

1. Write a series of personal questions on index cards. For example: "How old were you when you lost your virginity?" "Where did you first have sex?" "What's the worst thing you did as a kid?" "What's your secret fantasy?" "Which movie star do you have a secret crush on?" and so on.

2. On a second set of index cards, write a number of stunts for players to perform. For example: "Do ten sit-ups," "Make a loud burping sound," "Stand on your head for thirty seconds," "Remove one article of clothing," "Eat a banana dipped in peanut butter (or ketchup)," "Sing the *Phantom of the Opera* theme," and so on.

3. Place the question cards facedown in one pile, and place stunt cards facedown in a second pile.

4. Seat the players around the cards.

5. Have Player 1 draw a card from the question pile and read it aloud.

6. Tell Player 1 to either answer the question truthfully, or refuse to answer and pick a stunt card.

7. Once the question has been answered or the stunt completed, move on to Player 2, and so on, until all the question cards are gone.

Variation

Divide the group into two teams, and have each team make up questions and stunts for the opposing team.

TV Charades

TV junkies will love this variation of Charades. All the actions in this version are limited to the Boob Tube.

Materials Needed

- 40 index cards
- Pens or pencils
- Stopwatch or timer

Playing Time: 45–60 minutes

How to Play

1. Divide the players into two teams.

2. Give each team twenty index cards and some pens or pencils.

3. Tell the teams to go into separate rooms and to write down the names of twenty TV shows on the index cards.

4. When the teams have completed their cards, have them return to the game room and sit together with their teammates.

5. Place the cards in two piles in the center of the room.

6. Have Player 1 from Team 1 pick a card from Team 2's pile and silently read the name of the TV show.

7. Give Player 1 two minutes to act out the TV show title to Team 1.

8. If Team 1 guesses the name of the show within the time limit, write down the number of seconds it took them to guess the answer. If they don't guess, write the full two minutes.

9. Continue alternating teams and players until all the cards are gone.

10. Add up all the times for each team, and award a prize to the team with the fewest seconds.

Variation

Instead of using TV-show titles, allow players to write down TV stars, TV characters, TV slogans, and so on.

TV Morgue

The Lone Ranger, I Love Lucy, Gilligan's Island. Take a trip down memory lane, and see how well you remember those old show.

Materials Needed
• Paper and pencil to keep score

Playing Time: 30–45 minutes

How to Play
1. Gather the players in a circle.

2. Have Player 1 begin the game by saying the name of an old TV show, such as *Bonanza, M.A.S.H., The Flintstones,* or another favorite program.

3. Tell Player 1 to name one character from the old show. If the program selected is *Bonanza,* Player 1 may name Hoss.

4. Have the next player in the circle name another character from the show, such as Little Joe, for example.

5. Continue around the circle until a player cannot name another character from the selected show. At this point, open the play to the group. If someone else can still name another character from the show, the player who was stuck loses a point, and the player who called out another character earns a point.

6. When the round has ended, have the next player in line name another TV show and begin the game again. Continue until every player had a chance to name a show.

7. Award a prize to the player with the most points.

Variation
Using a TV source book, write down the names of obscure TV characters on index cards. Have players draw cards and try to name the show to which the character belongs. For example, if you write "Uncle Fester," the correct answer would be, "A character from *The Addams Family.*"

Twist and Shout

For this variation on the physically challenging game of Twister, your head must be as flexible as your body.

Materials Needed

- Twister game board, or a large cloth sheet or plastic shower curtain and markers
- Index cards
- Book of trivia questions

Playing Time: 30–45 minutes

How to Play

1. If you have a Twister game, all you need is the plastic game board. If you don't, make your own using a large cloth sheet or plastic shower curtain. Draw circles on the sheet and fill them in with red, blue, yellow, and green markers.

2. On index cards, write challenging (but not impossible) physical tasks associated with the colored circles, such as, "Place hand on yellow circle," "Place foot on blue circle," and "Place elbow on red circle."

3. On another set of index cards, write a variety of trivia questions. Keep the question pile and physical tasks pile separate.

4. Have Player 1 draw a card from the question pile and try to answer the trivia question. If the answer is correct, Player 1 doesn't have to do anything more. If the answer is incorrect, Player 1 must draw a card from the physical tasks pile and follow the instructions. Player 1 must hold his or her position until the next time he or she must answer a question.

5. Continue taking turns until a player falls, unable to keep his or her position.

Variation

Instead of stopping the game when someone falls, have the fallen player leave the game, and continue until only one player remains.

Undercover

Uma Thurman—is that her real name? What about Woody Allen? Emilio Estevez? John Wayne? Which stars have gone undercover?

Materials Needed

- Movie star trivia book, available at a library or bookstore
- Index cards
- Paper
- Pencils, 1 for each player

Playing Time: 30 minutes

How to Play

1. Find a book in the library that lists movie stars and their real names. For example: Woody Allen is really Allen Konigsberg, Tony Curtis is really Bernard Schwartz, Marilyn Monroe is really Norma Jean Baker, and so on.

2. Write the stars' real names on index cards, and stack them in a pile facedown.

3. Have the players draw cards and try to identify the movie star. Let the players keep the cards if they're correct.

4. Continue playing until all the cards are gone.

5. Award a prize to the player with the most cards.

Variation

Find out the middle or maiden names of your guests. Write the names on index cards. Have the players draw cards and guess who belongs to which name.

Under Pressure

How do stress and tension affect your game playing? Find out Under Pressure.

Materials Needed

• Items required for a variety of stunts (See Step 1.)
• Index cards
• Stopwatch or timer

Playing Time: 45–60 minutes

How to Play

1. Make a list of stunts for your players to perform. For example: "Eat an apple," "Braid someone's hair," "Write the alphabet," "Draw a cat," "Change your shoes," "Do the limbo," and so on.

2. Write the stunts on index cards, along with a time limit for performing each stunt.

3. Place cards facedown in a pile, easiest stunts on the top.

4. Have a player draw a card and perform the required stunt in the time indicated. For example, if the stunt says, "Eat an apple in thirty seconds," the player must try to complete that request in time. If the player succeeds, he or she gets a point.

5. Continue playing until everyone has completed a stunt. Add more stunts to make the game longer, and make them harder as the game progresses.

6. Award a prize to the player with the most points.

Variation

Have all the players do each stunt at the same time, as a race. Award a point to the player who completes the stunt first.

Venus and Mars

Is the gender gap widening or is that just your imagination? Find out when you play Venus and Mars.

Materials Needed

• Index cards
• Pens

Playing Time: 30–45 minutes

How to Play

1. Divide the players into two teams—one of men and one of women—and send them to separate rooms.

2. Give the teams index cards and pens, and ask them to write a series of gender-related stunts or questions. For example, the women may write, "Show us how to put on lipstick," "What is a bobbin?" "Demonstrate the correct way to put on panty hose," "What is Martha Stewart's area of expertise?" "How much does a newborn baby weigh?" "What is the Wonderbra?" and "Who is Mary Higgins Clark?" The men may write, "Show us how to tie a necktie," "What is a carburetor?" "Demonstrate the correct way to wear cuff links," "What is Bob Villa's area of expertise?" "How much does an average trout weigh?" "What is an athletic supporter?" and "Who is Elmore Leonard?"

3. After the cards are finished, have the teams sit on opposite sides of the room. Place the index cards in two piles in the center of the room.

4. Have a player from Team 1 select a card from Team 2's pile. Tell Team 1 to confer before answering. If Team 1 answers correctly, they get a point.

5. Continue alternating teams and questions until the cards are gone.

6. Award a prize to the team with the most points.

Variation

Instead of letting the teammates confer, have the player answer the question without assistance.

Wedding Night

This game is perfect for a wedding shower, but you can improvise and play any time you have a gathering of couples that includes gifts.

Materials Needed
- Wrapped gifts
- Paper
- Pen or pencil

Playing Time: 30 minutes

How to Play

1. Gather the guests around the pile of presents, and have the guest(s) of honor open the gifts.

2. Sit apart from the group and discreetly write the exclamations of the gift-opener that could be taken as sexual innuendoes, such as "Oh, it's so big!" "I've never seen one of these before!" "You have one of these too, don't you?" and "It's just my size!"

3. After all the gifts have been opened, get the group's attention and read the following aloud: "An ancient prophecy states that whatever a person says during gift-opening will be the very same words spoken on their wedding night."

4. Then read the comments you have written. You should have a collection of wonderfully funny and embarrassing statements that can be taken in a very naughty way!

Variation

Instead of applying this to the future wedding night, you can read the statements as they might have applied to a couple's "first time" by saying: "An ancient prophecy states that whatever a person says during gift-opening will be the very same words spoken during their very first time."

What the Heck is That?

Have you ever seen one of those weird-looking thingamabobs and wondered what it was? Here's your chance to find out!

Materials Needed
• Unusual gadgets, objects, thingamabobs
• Paper
• Pencils, 1 for each player

Playing Time: 30–45 minutes

How to Play

1. Find a bunch of odd-looking objects, or ask each guest to bring one odd object to the party.

2. Set the objects on the table and gather the players in a circle.

3. Distribute paper and pencils.

4. Present the first item, pass it around for each player to examine, and ask the players to write what they think the item is or what it does.

5. After all objects have been passed around, show each one again, and ask the players to read their answers for each one. You should get some funny answers.

6. After everyone has shared their answers, give the correct answer for each object. Give a point for each correct answer.

7. Award a thingamabob to the player with the most points.

Variation

Ask the players to bring an odd photograph to look at and identify, an unusual food to taste and identify, or a picture of an exotic location to identify.

What's Missing?

This game will make your guests feel like they're in the twilight zone. Everything appears normal, but something is not quite right!

Materials Needed

• Party supplies in keeping with your chosen theme
• Paper
• Pencils, 1 for each player

Playing Time: 45–60 minutes

How to Play

1. Choose a theme for your party—any theme you like—and decorate the party room accordingly, with decorations, name tags, place markers, place mats, table settings, centerpieces, serving dishes, food, utensils, favors, and so on.

2. Once the party room is all set, make twenty changes in the room. For example: remove an item here and there, such as someone's name tag, a place marker, or a place mat; add something different to the table setting, such as a serving dish not in keeping with your theme; serve foods in unusual ways, such as offering a finger food without toothpicks or placing a large fork in the soup tureen; make one of the favors different from the rest; and so on.

3. Invite the players into the party room and give each of them paper and a pencil. Tell them that twenty things are wrong with the room, and give them an hour to find them all.

4. Ask the players to discreetly write down their discoveries, and not to share them with the other players.

5. When the hour is up, have the players read their lists.

6. Award a prize to the player with the most finds.

Variation

Set up the party room and allow guests to view the area. Remove guests, then ask them to enter the room one at a time, change something in the room, and leave again. After every player had a chance to make one change, let all the players back into the room, and tell them to find all the changes.

What's the Meaning of This?!

If you're a good liar, you'll be a great at this game! If not, at least try to keep a straight face while you weave your tangled web.

Materials Needed

• Dictionary
• 50 index cards
• Pencils, 1 for each player

Playing Time: 30–45 minutes

How to Play

1. Look in the dictionary, and write down twenty unusual words and their definitions.

2. Write down thirty more unusual words, but do not include their definitions.

3. Shuffle the cards and place them in a pile.

4. Have the players sit in a circle and draw one card each. Give them a few minutes to study the written definition, or to create a definition if one is not given.

5. Have the players set their cards facedown. Then, one at a time, the players should say their words and definitions.

6. After each player explains the word, tell the other players to guess whether the player was lying or telling the truth, indicating with thumbs down or thumbs up.

7. Give a point to the player who catches another player in a lie. The player who read the definition gets a point for each player he or she fooled; this also applies to the player whose correct definition was pronounced false.

Variation

Instead of words, find a bunch of unusual items (around the house or at a dime store), such as a nose-hair plucker, a fuzzball shaver, or a bellybutton guard. Have the players take turns explaining the items' uses, honestly or creatively.

Where Are They Now?

What ever happened to Beaver Cleaver? Don Knotts? That kid in the Oscar Meyer Wiener commercial?

Materials Needed

- Book from the series "What ever happened to.." available at the library or bookstore
- 20 index cards
- Paper
- Pencils, 1 for each player

Playing Time: 30–45 minutes

How to Play

1. Write down the names of twenty of your favorite old stars on index cards—one name per card.

2. On a separate sheet of paper, write down what became of each star. Keep the answer sheet hidden.

3. Distribute paper and pencils.

4. Have one player draw a card and read the name of the former star.

5. Tell all the players to write down what they think happened to that once-famous person. You should get some funny answers.

6. After all the cards have been read, read them again, one at a time, and have the players read their guesses. Give a point for each correct answer.

7. Award a prize to the player with the most points.

Variation

Instead of using famous people, find out what happened to old friends instead.

Where Do They Come From?

Ever wonder where some of our everyday products come from? Take a guess and find out!

Materials Needed

• Book on where things come from, available at the library or book store
• Paper
• Pencils, 1 for each player

Playing Time: 30–45 minutes

How to Play

1. Research in the library or bookstore, and make a list of items whose origins you locate. If possible, collect the actual items on your list, such as guitar strings, baking soda, perfume, silly putty, mercury (in a thermometer), rat poison, dust bunnies, aluminum cans, chocolate, CDs, plastic vomit, and so on.

2. At game time, distribute paper and pencils.

3. Have the players sit in a circle.

4. Hold up one item for everyone to see, then pass it around the circle so each player can take a closer look.

5. Ask the players to write down the item's origin.

6. When all the items have been passed around, hold them up again, one at a time, and have the players read their answers.

7. Read the correct answers, and give a point for each correct answer.

8. Award a prize to the player with the most points.

Variation

Instead of asking about the items' origins, ask about their composition or ingredients.

Where's My Lawyer?

Have your day in court with a prosecuting attorney, defense attorney, jury, and, of course, the judge!

Materials Needed
- Synopsis of a fictional or real court case
- Index cards
- Appropriate costumes, badges, and decorations

Playing Time: 1 hour

How to Play

1. Use the library to help you create a fictional or real court case involving theft, extortion, blackmail, murder, or a sex scandal.

2. Write a synopsis of the case; photocopy the synopsis for all players.

3. Write down various court roles on index cards, including defendant, prosecuting attorney, defense attorney, judge, bailiff, and jury member.

4. Have each player draw a card to determine their court assignments. Provide costumes and have them dress accordingly. Give each player a name tag with that player's name and title, so everyone knows who's who.

5. Have the players take their places in court, then have the bailiff read the case aloud.

6. Begin the proceedings, and have the players make up their roles and speeches as they go along.

7. After the case has been presented, let the jury decide the outcome.

Variation

Use an old script from the *Perry Mason* TV show as the basis for your case, assign roles, and have the players act them out.

Where the Heck is Hackensack?

Do you know your home town like the back of your hand? Hey, where did that birthmark come from?!

Materials Needed

• 50 index cards
• Paper
• Pencils, 1 for each player (optional)

Playing Time: 30–45 minutes

How to Play

1. Research fifty facts about your local area, using library reference books, tourist maps, or Chamber of Commerce brochures.

2. Turn the fifty facts into questions, and write each question on an individual index card. You can make the questions open-ended, such as "What's New Jersey's nickname?" or multiple choice, such as "The New Jersey State Insect is the (a) bumblebee, (b) honeybee, (c) killer bee, (d) wannabe." Have fun with the questions, but make sure to include the correct answer.

3. Write the answer on the back of each card.

4. Have the players sit in a circle.

5. Read the questions to the group and have them race to give their answers. If you like, have them answer one at a time, moving around the circle, or have them all write down their answers.

6. Read the questions again, and then read the answers. Give a point for each correct answer.

7. Award a prize to the player with the most points.

Variation

Make the game national instead of local.

Who Am I . . . Not?

Is that Madonna arriving at the party? That can't be Mel Gibson behind those sunglasses, can it? Guess who!

Materials Needed

• Recognizable costume accessories of famous people, such as Madonna's metal cone-shaped bra, Mel Gibson's kilt from *Braveheart,* Glenn Close's two-toned wig from *101 Dalmatians,* Fabio's long locks and shirt open to the waist, and so on
• Paper
• Pencils, 1 for each player

Playing Time: 30 minutes

How to Play

1. Collect costume accessories from thrift and second-hand stores.

2. Ask guests to select something from the costume bag and put it on.

3. Distribute paper and pencils.

4. When everyone is dressed in their costumes, have the players guess who each player is supposed to be.

5. Tell them to write down their answers.

6. When all players have guessed, ask each player to identify the costumed character. Give a point for each correct answer.

7. Award a prize to the player with the most points.

Variation

Have players dress as one another, then have them guess who's who.

Whoops! There It Goes!

Are you sticky fingers or butterfingers? Try to pass "it" along without going "whoops!"

Materials Needed

• Pairs of unusual items to pass along, such as full cups of water, snails or slugs, slices of pizza, pieces of confetti, slightly cracked raw eggs, sticky candy, Gak or Slime, oily balls, and so on

Playing Time: 30 minutes

How to Play

1. Prepare unusual and challenging items to be passed along in a line, and place them on a table in two lines, in the same order.

2. Divide players into two teams, and have each team stand in a line.

3. Have the first players in each line take the first item and pass it to the next player.

4. As soon as an item reaches the end of the line, have the last player bring it back to the front, set it on the table, and take another item to be passed down the line.

5. If a player drops an item, have the team start again with that same item. (You may want to line the floor with plastic and have backups for the cups of water and the eggs!)

6. Award a prize to the team that finishes passing all items first.

Variation

Have players wear oversized gloves when they pass things along, to make the game more challenging. Or have them pass things with their eyes closed. (See Pass the Pretzel, page 105, and Scoop-a-Cup, page 128, for other variations on this game.)

Wine Tasting Game

Host a wine-tasting party that doubles as a game. Smell the bouquet, sip the heady flavor, and name that wine!

Materials Needed

- Bottles of wine
- Brown paper bags or aluminum foil
- Wine glasses, 1 for each player
- Paper
- Pencils, 1 for each player

Playing Time: 2 hours

How to Play

1. Assign each guest to bring a specific bottle of red or white wine, wrapped in a paper bag or aluminum foil so the name cannot be identified. Be sure to include a number of varieties. For example, for red wine, have merlot, zinfandel, cabernet, and pinot noir.

2. Collect the wine as guests arrive, and place them on the table in no particular order.

3. Select the first bottle at random, and pour a small amount into each player's wine glass.

4. Allow players time to sample and enjoy the taste of the wine. If you like, hand out sheets of wine-tasting tips your guests can use as a guide.

5. Distribute paper and pencils.

6. Have guests write down what kind of wine they think it is.

7. Offer food between tastes, and provide a spittoon for the players who don't want to finish their samples.

8. When everyone has guessed, reveal the label and see who identified the wine correctly.

Variation

Use a variety of favorite and obscure beers instead of wine.

Yearbook

It's shocking to see how much we've changed over the years, especially when compared to our high-school graduation photos!

Materials Needed
- Players' high-school graduation photos
- Paper
- Pencils, 1 for each player

Playing Time: 30 minutes

How to Play

1. Ask guests to mail their high-school graduation photos to you before the party.

2. Enlarge the photos at a copy store to 5-by-7-inch size, so they're easily visible.

3. Mount the photos on construction paper. Under each picture, write real or fictional information about the person, such as "Most likely to sleep her way to the top," "Class nerd," "Voted best looking in a snowsuit," and so on.

4. Hang the photos on the wall.

5. At game time, distribute paper and pencils.

6. Have the players examine the photos and try to guess who's who. Tell them to write down their answers.

7. When everyone has guessed, have each player identify his or her photo. Give a point for each correct guess.

8. Award a prize to the player with the most points.

Variation

Draw disguises on the photocopies, and write false clues to their identities underneath the pictures.

You Must Have Been a Beautiful Baby!

'Cause, baby, look at you now! Can you guess who that cute kid is? The drooling one with no teeth or hair?

Materials Needed

• Baby pictures of players
• Construction paper
• Paper
• Pencils, 1 for each player

Playing Time: 30 minutes

How to Play

1. Call guests a few days before the party, and ask them to mail you a photocopy or a print of one of their baby pictures.

2. Mount the pictures on construction paper.

3. At game time, have the players sit in a circle.

4. Distribute paper and pencils.

5. Pass around each photo, one at a time.

6. Ask players to write down their guesses as to who each beautiful baby is.

7. When everyone has guessed every picture, hold up the pictures one at a time, and have each grown-up baby identify his or her picture. Give a point for each correct guess.

8. Award a prize to the player with the most points.

Variation

Instead of using pictures of the players, find baby pictures or high-school pictures of celebrities, and have players identify them.

The Best Party Book

by Penny Warner

This party-planning book provides creative ideas for invitations, decorations, refreshments, games, prizes, and party favors to turn your parties into memorable celebrations. Includes ideas for seasonal parties (Halloween, Christmas, and more), family events (birthdays, anniversaries, and more), and special TV events (the Academy Awards and the Super Bowl).

Order #6089 $8.00

The Kids' Pick-A-Party Book

by Penny Warner
Illustrated by Laurel Aiello

Here are 50 creative theme parties to make birthdays and other celebrations fun. Warner provides themed ideas for invitations, decorations, costumes, games, activities, food, and party favors to help parents make celebrations memorable and entertaining.

Order #6090 $9.00   Available February '98

Kids' Party Cookbook

by Penny Warner
Illustrated by Laurel Aiello

Over 175 reduced-fat recipes with food that's fun and tasty for kids but full of nutrition to please parents. Warner has fun ideas for every meal, including mini-meals, such as Peanut Butter Burger Dogs and Twinkle Sandwiches, and creative snacks, such as Aquarium Jell-O and Prehistoric Bugs. (Ages 8 and up)

Order #2435 $12.00

Kids' Holiday Fun

by Penny Warner
Illustrated by Kathy Rogers

You will find fun ideas for entertaining your children during 34 holidays, including New Year's, Valentine's Day, St. Patrick's Day, Fourth of July, Halloween, and Christmas. Turn to this comprehensive guide for delicious holiday recipes, decoration suggestions, instructions for fun holiday activities and games, party ideas, and crafts.

Order #6000 $12.00

Order Form

Qty.	Title	Author	Order No.	Unit Cost (U.S. $)	Total
	Age Happens	Lansky, B.	4025	$7.00	
	Are You Over the Hill?	Dodds, B.	4265	$7.00	
	Best Baby Shower Book	Cooke, C.	1239	$7.00	
	Best Baby Shower Game Book	Cooke, C.	6063	$3.95	
	Best Birthday Party Game Book	Lansky, B.	6064	$3.95	
	Best Bridal Shower Game Book	Cooke, C.	6060	$3.95	
	Best Couple's Shower Game Book	Cooke, C.	6061	$3.95	
	Best Party Book	Warner, P.	6089	$8.00	
	Best Wedding Shower Book	Cooke, C.	6059	$7.00	
	Familiarity Breeds Children	Lansky, B.	4015	$7.00	
	For Better And For Worse	Lansky, B.	4000	$7.00	
	Games People Play	Warner, P.	6093	$8.00	
	How to Survive Your 40th Birthday	Dodds, B.	4260	$6.00	
	Italian without Words	Cangelosi/Carpini	5100	$6.00	
	Just for Fun Party Game Book	Warner, P.	6065	$3.95	
	Kids' Holiday Fun	Warner, P.	6000	$12.00	
	Kids' Party Cookbook	Warner, P.	2435	$12.00	
	Kids' Party Games and Activities	Warner, P.	6095	$12.00	
	Kids' Pick-A-Party Book	Warner, P.	6090	$9.00	
	Lovesick	Lansky, B.	4045	$7.00	
	Over-the-Hill Party Game Book	Cooke, C.	6062	$3.95	
	Pick A Party	Sachs, P.	6085	$9.00	
	What's So Funny/Getting Old?	Noland, J.	4205	$7.00	
				Subtotal	
			Shipping and Handling (see below)		
			MN residents add 6.5% sales tax		
				Total	

YES! Please send me the books indicated above. Add $2.00 shipping and handling for the first book and 50¢ for each additional book. Add $2.50 to total for books shipped to Canada. Overseas postage will be billed. Allow up to four weeks for delivery. Send check or money order payable to Meadowbrook Press. No cash or C.O.D's please. Prices subject to change without notice. **Quantity discounts available upon request.**

Send book(s) to:

Name _____ Address _____

City _____ State _____ Zip _____

Telephone (_____)_____ P.O. number (if necessary) _____

Payment via:

❏ Check or money order payable to Meadowbrook Press (No cash or C.O.D.'s please)
  Amount enclosed $ _____
❏ Visa (for orders over $10.00 only)   ❏ MasterCard (for orders over $10.00 only)
Account # _____ Signature _____ Exp. Date _____

A FREE Meadowbrook Press catalog is available upon request.
You can also phone us for orders of $10.00 or more at 1-800-338-2232.

Mail to: Meadowbrook Press
5451 Smetana Drive, Minnetonka, MN 55343

Phone (612) 930-1100   Toll -Free 1-800-338-2232   Fax (612) 930-1940